Remodeling
Your Bathroom

Remodeling Your Bathroom

by Patrick Galvin

Drawings by
Dick Meyer and Ray Pioch

POPULAR SCIENCE BOOKS

HARPER & ROW, PUBLISHERS

NEW YORK

LIBRARY OF CONGRESS CATALOG CARD NUMBER: 79-91444
ISBN: 0-06-090780-0

Manufactured in the United States of America

Cover setting courtesy *Baths by Royal*

Contents

Introduction

THE HISTORY of bathrooms has been a cyclical type of development that can be traced back as far as 4,000 years. In succession thay have been public, private, communal, for kings and nobles only, constructed of beautiful marble and pieced together with bark and mud.

But 90 percent of all the progress in bathroom function and design through all of these many centuries has been effected in the last 25 years! So if your bathroom is 25 years old it might as well be 100 years old, and it is not much more modern than if it had been designed and built 1,000 years ago.

So, now that you are going to do something about your bathroom, it would be prudent to consider what will make it really modern and in tune with new developments in materials and design.

There are these primary considerations.

• It probably will need a complete remodeling, not simply replacement of fixtures.

• Your remodeling plans should be aimed at gaining adequate space for the functions and activities you want to take place there.

• You should think in terms of an integrated design that will include space planning for storage, for activities, and for visual appeal, with harmonious combinations of materials, textures and colors.

In this book we advise you on how to do all of these things yourself. But we also suggest you call on experts, and we guide you on how to identify the experts.

It is important to remember that *knowing how* to do something does not necessarily mean you *can* do it. What the mind knows is often difficult to transmit to the hands that guide the tools. And errors or slips can be very costly. If you should accidentally drop a new wall cabinet on a newly-installed Corian vanity top, for example, that's $500 to $1,000 down the drain. This is simply to point out what you probably already realize: A good do-it-yourself job requires care, caution and thought.

In addition, keep in mind the realities of the '80s while planning your new bathroom. Think in terms of water conservation, and of fuel-efficient heat and hot water. Think in terms of cleanability, of safety, and of durability. Think also in terms of your family's changing needs in the future. And think in terms of really getting value for your dollar. This is a major undertaking, and an expensive one. So make sure it is done right.

And then go to it, for a happier, cheerier, more comfortable rest-of-your-life!

PAT GALVIN

1 | Your Present Bathroom

BATHROOM PROBLEMS often are like old shoe problems. You get so used to them that you don't realize the nail has worked through until you feel the callus. You don't know about the hole in the sole until someone remarks on it.

But think about it. Do you have to squint to accomplish simple grooming tasks?

Do you bump your head on a medicine cabinet when you try to wash your hair in the sink?

Do you sometimes knock your knee or your shin on the toilet, or your elbow on the wall of the shower? Do you slip in the tub?

Do you sometimes have to leave the bathroom to go to a closet for a clean towel, or more toilet paper?

Do you have to schedule your bathroom time in the mornings to avoid conflicts with other family members?

If you have experienced any one or more of these problems, don't think you are alone. Any average American (or German or Frenchman or anyone else) could double or triple that list with ease. Right now there are thousands of bathrooms all over this country that have steam on the mirrors, mildew that must be cleaned from the caulking around the tub, deteriorating wallcovering from excessive humidity, shivering occupants, and inadequate storage space.

Do you deserve all this?

No, you don't! Chances are that you had absolutely nothing to do with the design of your bathroom. It was designed by a builder, or by his architect, and neither of them had any idea of your personal habits, of the number in your family or of what improvements you would be willing to pay for. A builder has to build and design for averages. But are you average? Do you have 2½ children?

Besides that, the passage of the years does to a bathroom what it does to all of us. But while we might be able to age gracefully, a bathroom is not so adaptable; it can only wear out.

There is something else that happens to a bathroom as time goes by. It not only deteriorates with age. It also becomes dated by new conveniences, new materials, new products that were not available in the home only a dozen years ago.

For example, there now is new cabinetry engineered especially for the bathroom, large or small. There are countertops made of cultured marble, a man-made material, with integral sink bowl molded in. There are tubs, shower stalls and their surrounds fashioned of molded fiberglass, with molded-in seats, soap dishes, grab-bars, and shelves. There are tubs with built-in whirlpool water jets, and separate whirlpool units

Cabinets engineered for the bathroom are now available, such as these by Poggenpohl, a German manufacturer. Other makers include Allibert of France and Quaker Maid here in the U.S.

that can be attached to the side of your old tub. You can, with relative ease, add a steam bath. Bathrooms are being expanded to include sauna, exercise rooms, laundry, housekeeping centers, and one manufacturer even offers a home spa (somewhat larger than a bathtub placed in the wall sideways) that can, at the push of a button, give you desert sun, evening rain, sauna, steam or shower in outrageous luxury.

You also can buy a tub or shower stall of cultured marble and use matching material on the walls. You can buy faucets and accessories in crystal or crystal-like acrylic, or in bronze, pewter or gold, or in a colorful ceramic. You can buy faucets, showerheads and toilets that save water. You can get a single unit for the ceiling that heats, lights and ventilates the room. You can buy ceramic tile that applies right over the old for a new look, and that comes in pre-grouted sheets for easy application.

And if you really are energy-conscious, you even can avoid use of the basement storage-type water heater by installing small, local, coil-type water heaters that heat no water until you use it, and then heat only what you use.

So the modern bathroom obviously is not the strictly utilitarian facility it used to be, with three fixtures, four walls and a door.

One recent development is the Jacuzzi whirlpool. These tubs come in a range of sizes: the smallest replaces a standard bathtub; the largest holds five or six people at a time. There are also several other manufacturers of this type of tub.

Because of modern lifestyles, new products, new materials and raised consciousness it now can be a beautiful and pleasant room, easy to clean and to keep clean.

A remodeled bathroom can add great value and sales appeal to a home you want to sell. But its real value is in the home you want to live in: in the day-to-day convenience it provides, and in the removal of a source of family friction.

RATING YOUR PRESENT BATHROOM. Everything about your present bathroom is either great or terrible, or somewhere in between. But just how good is it, or how bad?

Here's a way to add up the score in a way that can, perhaps, influence your decision on whether to put your money into a remodeling project.

Read each question, consider it, then rate your bathroom. If the answer is "Terrible," or "No," circle number 1. If it is "Great," or "Yes," circle number 5. The midpoint, 3, would be "Acceptable," not bad and not good.

1. General condition. What kind of shape is it in? Are the fixtures chipped, or the walls cracked? Are you proud of it when your friends visit? Do you feel it would be an asset if you were selling your home?   1 2 3 4 5

2. Esthetics. Whether it is conservative traditional in style or wild contemporary, does it
look good?

1 2 3 4 5

3. Function. Does it have elbow room
where you need it? Is it adequate for the family? Does it have enough mirrors in the right
places? Is it safe for all members of the family?
Are the razor blades and the Sani-Flush out of
reach of children? Does the tub have a slip-
resistant surface, and are grab-bars provided?

1 2 3 4 5

4. Storage. Is there space for toiletries, towels, papers, cleaning materials, and all the
things you think should be in the bathroom?

1 2 3 4 5

5. Lighting. Can you really see adequately
for what you do there? Can you see to read the
small print? Can you see to make up properly?
And is the light where you want it to be?

1 2 3 4 5

6. Ventilation. Are odors removed in reasonable time? Is the mirror free of steam when
you emerge from a hot shower?

1 2 3 4 5

7. Heat. Is it comfortable in the winter? In
the morning, or after a hot bath?

1 2 3 4 5

8. Cleanability. Does the whole room clean
easily with little more than a damp sponge?
Are grout lines free of mildew? Can you clean
both floors and walls in only a few minutes?

1 2 3 4 5

9. Modernity. Does the bathtub have sleek,
modern lines, or does it stand on clawed feet?
Do you pull a chain to flush the toilet? Is
plumbing concealed behind a wall or cabinet
or is it exposed under the sink? Are the walls
covered with moisture-proof materials, or is
there nothing but paint on all the walls, including those around the tub?

1 2 3 4 5

10. Energy/Conservation Consciousness. Is
the room heated only as needed, or is it always
over-heated in winter? Have any flow-restric-
tors been used in faucets, showerhead? Is the
hot water just adequate, or is it hotter than it
need be? If there is a window, is it tight and
well-caulked? Is there a storm window? Does
the toilet use water sparingly?

1 2 3 4 5

11. Privacy. Do you really feel you are in a private place when you close the door, or can you hear everything that goes on in the next room?

1 2 3 4 5

Now add your scores and total here: _____

If your score is

11-16: Your bathroom is a disaster. Forget the vacation in Mexico and put the money into your bathroom, and figure a minimum of $2,000.

17-29: You've got problems, and they are serious. But you can do a lot with $1,500, if you do much of the work yourself.

30-39: This is in the "adequate" range, and it might be close to being pretty good. Your danger in this range is the temptation to do patchwork remodeling. Be sure you make an integrated plan to tie it all together in a designed package. You can probably do it all yourself.

40-48: About all you need are cosmetic changes, probably. Look into the new materials available and plan to do it yourself. And be sure you anchor those grab-bars into the studs.

40-55: Congratulations. Have a good time in Mexico.

INITIAL PLANNING. The first step in any bathroom remodeling project is planning. Don't go out and buy anything, however much you might like it, until you have figured out carefully the adequacy of present facilities and the shortcomings, and the new activities you would like to include. Remember that a modern bathroom is a coordinated package, not just a collection of items.

So, as a first step in planning, visit a bathroom showroom where complete bathrooms are on display, and visit a large bathroom boutique where you can see a wide selection of accessory items. Normally you will find the best complete bathroom displays in the showrooms of the better kitchen dealers of your area. The better boutiques in an area might be separate shops or they might be in department stores. If you aren't thrilled by what you see, look further. Each step is important, and deserves your time.

Be sure you see examples of sunken tubs, raised tubs, of cultured marble and Corian walls, of tile and innovative use of plastic laminates (such as the familiar Formica), of whirlpools (such as the Jacuzzi); and look for creative use of cabinetry in small and large bathroom displays. If you don't find all of these, keep looking until you do, because you can't develop the bathroom you want until you are familiar with what is available.

While this search is going on, invest in several of the newest magazines that feature home planning and design. Particularly, look for the ones featuring bathroom ideas on their covers. Check these out for products, materials and ideas, but consider them realistically because many of them feature bathrooms that would fit only in a palace.

Making Lists. As a second step in planning, sit down with a pencil and paper, and put a few things in writing. First make a list of all of the things that are wrong with your present bathroom. If you have more than one, make a separate list for each.

Be specific. Is the floor hard to clean? Is the tub hard to clean? Is the tub too slippery? Is the caulk line around the tub, where it meets the wall, mildewed? Is the lavatory large enough? Is it old and chipped? Is there counter surface, and is it enough? Is there storage for towels? For soaps? For your various cosmetics or vanity items? Is lighting adequate and in the right places? And so on.

Don't fail to write something down because you think it is not correctable. By the time you finish this book you may find solutions to these problems.

Now make another list of everything you want in your new bathroom. Again, don't hold back. Don't fail to write it down because you think it is too expensive, or that it won't fit. Write it all down.

After you've had a chance to make these lists, bring in the other family members and get their opinions. Write them all down. A bathroom is a family affair.

Measuring and Sketching. Now, using either a steel tape or a folding carpenter's rule, measure your existing bathroom. Make a sketch of each wall showing measurements, lighting, wall outlets, doors and windows.

On a window wall, measure from the end of the wall to the window framing, then the framing, the window itself, then the remainder of the wall. Make an overall measurement, and be sure it is the same as the total of the parts. Measure also from floor to ceiling showing also the dimensions of window and framing, and put all of these figures in your sketch. Do the same for any wall with a door in it, or any offsets there might be for a chimney or plumbing or ductwork, or a radiator.

It may be that you will turn this entire job over to a professional bathroom designer. If so, the designer will do all the measuring and sketching and planning. But you will be a more informed and knowledgeable customer if you take the trouble to measure, sketch and do some planning yourself first. You also will have a much more realistic concept of what you can expect, of what might be possible or impossible.

Other Questions. Now, in this initial planning of your bathroom remodeling, here are some of the questions you must ask — and answer.

• Are the present bathroom facilities enough for the family? Any family group of two should have at least one complete bathroom plus a half-bath. The need for a second facility moves up in importance if there are occasional parties. The bathroom plus the half-bath also can accommodate a family of three. But a family of four will need one complete bathroom plus two half-baths, or even better, a master bathroom, a secondary bathroom and a half-bath.

• Are the present bathroom facilities suitable for the ages of the family members? If there's a baby coming you might want a special lav in which it can be bathed. A toddler can't cope with grown-up heights and you might want a lowered counter section with a second lav. Will aged parents be moving in with you who need special safety features?

• Must you allow for any handicapped persons? You can plan things now that can make life a lot easier for them and for whoever must care for them.

• Are there activities you want to do in the bathroom, but can't? This might include making up in the morning or evening, or laundry collection, possibly the entire laundry operation. If you have been thinking of a health and exercise program, can you design the equipment into the bathroom or an adjacent room? Do you want a steambath? How about a sauna? A sauna can go elsewhere, but it goes best in the bathroom area. If you'd like the laundry in the bathroom, can you expand it into a housekeeping center to include sewing and other clothing care?

• Now, think big. Is there adjacent space to the present bathroom into which it can be expanded?

Make sure you have all of your questions written down. Now we can start looking for answers.

2 | What Can You Do About It?

THE NEXT QUESTIONS are: What can you do about it? What will you do about it? And here you have a lot of options.

If you simply want the bathroom to look better, you can opt for the easiest and least costly choice of redecorating it. At the other end of the scale, your option will be full-scale remodeling, which might include new wiring, new plumbing and removal of a wall. This could be costly, but it also would return the greatest benefits.

There are a lot of choices in between. Let's consider these from the viewpoint of the nature of the problem.

THE NEED FOR MORE STORAGE SPACE

1. Add a bathroom vanity cabinet. The most basic ones, found in home centers, are just boxes that hide the plumbing. But the better ones have drawers, shelves, hampers and interior fittings to accommodate towels, wash cloths, dirty clothes, cleaning materials and waste. Better vanity cabinets come in units that combine with other units, so they can be expanded to fill the available space.

The better manufacturers of vanity cabinets make them in several sizes and types, with drawer, shelf, and hamper units. They're designed so you can combine several units to build up what you need.

Chemcraft Inc.

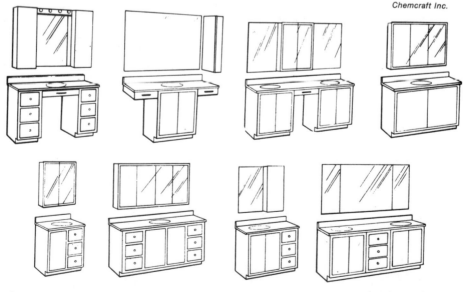

Add other cabinets. There's more available than just vanity and medicine cabinets. These are French, by Allibert. In the U.S., Quaker Maid makes special cabinets for the bathroom.

2. Add other types of cabinets. For example, linen cabinets are made for the bathroom by kitchen cabinet manufacturers in 3″ modular widths ranging from as little as 15″ wide to 42″ wide. Or you can build one yourself or have a carpenter do it. Special "families" of cabinets have been engineered for bathroom use by Quaker Maid, which has dealers nationwide; by Poggenpohl, a German brand widely distributed here; by Hafa, a Swedish brand with limited availability; and by Allibert, a French brand also with limited availability. (See Appendix for manufacturers' addresses.) There also are smaller cabinet/shelving assemblies available through Sears and similar sources that fit over the toilet tank, on counters or in corners, and on the floor. You can buy shallow cabinets to fit on the door or in the wall between the studs.

3. Borrow space from adjacent rooms. For example, there might be a closet behind one bathroom wall. It is a bit complicated, but it is possible to go through the wall, cutting out the studs and framing the opening, to expand the bathroom into the former closet. If you need the closet space, consider adding a closet elsewhere in the room. It usually is easier to add a closet (even a wardrobe might suffice) than to gain space for the bathroom any other way. If there is no closet to borrow, you might have a carpenter move a wall to make the bathroom bigger, the adjacent room smaller. But such structural changes can be expensive.

4. Change the floorplan. A builder usually arranges an upstairs bathroom so the plumbing and waste lines are in line with the kitchen, or with a downstairs bathroom, because it is economical and the sensible way to do it. But it can result in a floorplan that is inefficient in use of space, that does not allow for cabinets for storage. Changing the placement of fixtures will be expensive because of plumbing changes, but it also might provide the needed solution to gain space for cabinets. (See Chapter 7.)

THE NEED FOR IMPROVED FUNCTION

1. Provide a special place for children. For example, if there are young children who can't reach the lav at its customary 30″ height and who, if provided a stool, could get into the wrong medicines, you can lower a 15″ section of countertop by about 6″, put in a children's lav and, in the wall, a children's medicine cabinet. If this is done on the same wall as the regular lav it would be relatively easy to plumb it with the new plastic piping, and it can be done even in the usual small 5′x7′ bathroom.

2. Provide for the aged, infirm or handicapped. Here it would depend on the nature of the problem, but in any case the first thought would be for the addition of grab-bars for safety, and in a change from the old, slippery-bottom tub to one of the new models of "soft" fiberglass-reinforced plastic, with non-skid bottom, and molded-in seat and ledges.

The problem here is in getting the old tub out, and you would have to consider door and window measurements to figure if this is possible. Tubs go in easily when a house is being built. The new fiberglass models are made in one piece for new housing, but in three or four pieces for replacement. Skilled contractors have little trouble removing the framing of a window to get an old tub out.

3. Improve the lighting. This is a frequent cause of malfunction. The Light for Living standards, updated in 1979 by the American Home Lighting Institute, recommend good mirror lighting in a small bathroom with multiple bulbs totaling 120 to 180 watts, or 40 to 60 watts fluorescent. Suggested are luminous fixtures 28″ to 36″ apart, centered 60″ above the floor for good grooming; or suspended fixtures with 60 to 100 watts in each. A larger bathroom should have an added ceiling light with 100 to 150 watts incandescent or 60 to 80 watts fluorescent. The standards also suggest a ceiling light or wall bracket with 60 to 75 watts or 30 to 40 watts fluorescent for a toilet compartment. (See Chapter 12.)

Another possibility is a skylight; it might surprise you how easy it is to install one, even if there is an attic above.

4. Add other activities. This is a function of space, and there's no way you'll get an exercise room into a 5′x6′ bathroom. But think about it. Perhaps the children are grown and gone, and there's no longer any need for that fourth or third bedroom adjacent to the bathroom. Tearing out a wall would provide an ideal opportunity for exercise equipment, a housekeeping center with laundry and sewing facilities, a dressing area, perhaps even one of those spa units we mentioned earlier. These spa units by Kohler come in two sizes, the "Environment," 107″ long, and the "Habitat," 84″ long. On a more limited basis, you could get enough

Improved lighting. Skylights are surprisingly easy to install.

space for an exercise room or a laundry or a dressing room by incorporating a walk-in closet that might be adjacent to the bathroom. For a small family, a surprisingly small 24"x24" space can be adequate for a clothes washer and dryer, using small models developed for this purpose that stack on top of each other.

5. Improve heat and ventilation. Many bathrooms suffer from too little heat, and most suffer from too little ventilation. Both are relatively simple to improve. An electric baseboard can provide heat. So can the "Intertherm," a 1,000-watt hot-water unit that heats electrically, with a fan to supply the fast heat needed in the bathroom. This unit is notable because it can fit in the kick space under the vanity. Companies such as Broan, NuTone and others make ceiling and wall fixtures that provide both heat and ventilation, and light if you need it. The thing to consider in bathroom heat is that it can be a waste of energy to keep the space

Make it easier to clean. This tub and tub surround is all one piece, of fiberglass with acrylic surface. It wipes clean with a damp rag.

heated all the time. An infra-red heat lamp does not heat the entire room, but makes you feel warm when you are within its range. As for ventilation, if your mirrors steam up when you take a hot shower, the bathroom probably is under-ventilated. But a ventilating unit must have air to exhaust, and very often the steam-up problem is caused by a lack of air supply in the room. It often can be corrected by trimming an inch off the bottom of the bathroom door. It might also be necessary to have a nearby window open a crack to provide enough air. To prevent steam-up, it always is necessary to close the shower area off from the rest of the bathroom while the hot shower is running, with a shower curtain or sliding doors. If all else fails, replace the vent fan or blower with a more powerful unit. Remember, the high humidity evidenced by steam-up can be very damaging.

6. Replace the tub surround. If it is difficult to clean, this is a function failure. The space-age materials available today are easy to install and require practically no maintenance. Excellent materials for the three wall sections that make up a tub surround include plastic laminates, cultured marble, fiberglass and ceramic tile. You can buy plastic laminate kits with special corner moldings that are not difficult to assemble, or you can

Plastic laminate surfaces are easily kept clean, and very durable. This vanity cabinet has top of Wilsonart laminate, with matching laminate on doors and drawers.

A rejuvenated powder room. Wall covering is "Waverley Cycles" by J. Josephson, of humidity-proof vinyl, pre-pasted for do-it-yourself installation. Cultured marble top on vanity cabinet has two integral lav bowls.

find it in a single, continuous sheet bent at the two interior corners. A special material is DuPont's Corian, a man-made marble-like material that is unique in that it is machinable with power woodworking tools. This, too, comes in kit form for the bathroom, although you might want to add a molding at the top because it is a bit shorter than the standard framing of sliding tub doors. For instructions on installing these kits and materials, see Chapter 9.

THE NEED FOR IMPROVED APPEARANCE

1. **Put in new walls.** You can use any of the materials suggested for a tub surround. You might want a good vinyl wallcovering or redwood plank, or a humidity-resistant paneling. Or you can use paint. Just remember that if you darken the walls they will absorb light, so you may need more wattage.

2. **Change the ceiling.** It is relatively easy to install new ceiling tile, and you can work wonders and solve both an appearance and a lighting problem with a suspended luminous ceiling (see Chapter 11). You can also have a mirrored ceiling with a new lightweight glass substitute called Mirrorlite, although it might be a bit expensive for a purely decorative touch. Or, there is paint, vinyl wallcovering or plastic laminate.

3. **Change the floor.** You can install ceramic tile over the old floor, or stick-on squares in wood or resilient vinyl, or kitchen carpeting (not the same as indoor-outdoor carpet, although many salesmen think it is), or resilient sheet vinyl.

4. **Put in a new counter with integral bowl.** This might be of cultured marble or Corian. It can change or dramatize the color scheme, and add utility and cleanability. The counter can extend along an entire wall; it need not be limited to the size of the vanity cabinet beneath. Or simply install a new plastic laminate countertop to change the bathroom's appearance. (See Chapter 8.) Remember that dark surfaces absorb light and may necessitate more wattage.

5. **Change the medicine cabinet.** The builder usually puts in the most basic model and it goes unchanged forever. A really useful one will have three doors and three mirrors so you can see the back of your head. This type has added capacity, and often its own lighting either above or on both sides. There are compartmented models for toothbrushes, cosmetics, and so forth, and some even have a locking compartment for dangerous medicines.

6. **Check the accessory market for new products and designs.** You can find, for example, accessories in clear or colored Lucite, ceramic, and metals of various types. In some areas there are kitchen/bath dealers who have found imported tiles and had them matched in toilet seats and towel sets. Most of these are not cheap, but they can make magic in a bathroom.

3 | Contracting and Do-It-Yourself Options

SOONER OR LATER, the subject of money always comes up.

And, in this case, it might as well be sooner because most of us are uninformed of the costs involved in good products and skilled labor.

We might know what a plumber or electrician's basic hourly wage is. What we often fail to realize is that the contractor who employs him must get 40 to 60% more than that to arrange for the work, and to pay his taxes, rent, and all the other costs of doing business. Labor makes up more than 60% of any bathroom remodeling job, materials the rest. So the more we can do ourselves, the more money we save. But we will have to make up that percentage in our own time spent, and in blisters and skinned knuckles.

The products we will want keep increasing in price not only because it takes costly materials, machines and labor to make them, but because they often are greatly improved and are worth a lot more.

So the first thing to do is to establish ballpark figures for what we want to do, then make peace with ourselves for spending the money.

Most full-scale bathroom remodeling projects done entirely by a custom kitchen/bath dealer cost between $5,000 and $10,000. This includes tear-out of the old, replacement of the three basic fixtures with new ones, new tub or shower surround, faucets and shower head, vanity cabinet, countertop and sink, medicine cabinet, lighting, and proper treatment of floor, walls and ceiling. It includes changes in plumbing and wiring, all at professional rates and, of course, the dealer is a design professional.

At the other end of the scale you can buy the three basic fixtures in white at Sears for less than $200. You can buy plastic laminated countertop on special sale for a few dollars per lineal foot, in lengths of 4', 6', 8', 10' or 12'. You can find a basic vanity cabinet for less than $30. Cushioned vinyl sheet flooring can be found for less than a dollar per square foot and ceramic tile for slightly more.

A recent survey of dealers showed an "average" consumer expenditure for bathroom remodeling of, rounded off, $3,000. But average figures are not very meaningful for individual comparison. That average covered everything from simple replacement of a vanity top to full-scale remodeling jobs.

What you must do is come to grips, realistically, with what things you can do yourself and, if you wish, with the help of friends.

Here are some of the things you can and can't do — probably, remembering that sometimes the hands are inept no matter how much the brain knows.

You can do the basic plumbing for installation of fixtures, with the guidance you will find in Chapter 7.

You can't relocate waste and vent stacks unless you are an expert.

You can do the basic electrical work.

You can't run entirely new wiring from the fuse box or circuit breaker, unless you are an expert.

And you can't do either plumbing or electrical work without a permit and inspection by the local authority, unless you are in a rural area where there are no codes.

You can do all the tear-out of the old.

You can't tear out a cast-iron tub by yourself. These weigh anywhere from 250 to 500 pounds, and they are a real problem even for the pros. You can identify a cast-iron tub by the solid thunk you hear when you pound it, or by the fact that there is no bending of the bottom when you stand in it. A steel tub might be very difficult to remove, but it also can be cut to smaller pieces with a hacksaw. It will have a drummy sound when you knock on the bottom.

You can resurface an old tub, in white or any color, and make it look like new, if you are very careful about following directions that come with the resurfacing kit. Thus you can match the tub color to the color of a new toilet and sink.

You can install ceramic tile, cultured marble and plastic laminate (see Chapters 8, 9 and 10).

You can install a skylight, even with an attic above.

You can't install a skylight for a first-floor interior bathroom with no outside walls, if it is a two-story house or more.

You can install a suspended ceiling, luminous or not, to lower an old-style high ceiling.

You can open an existing wall to expand the bathroom.

You can't, however, open a wall containing ductwork or plumbing, without rerouting those. Putting more elbows in ductwork will diminish your heating or cooling airflow. You also will have to be careful not to destroy any load-bearing function of the wall by adding framing.

You can install paneling or wallboard. You can paint. You can hang wallcovering. You can use tools.

You can, in short, do just about everything to remodel your own bathroom, or to add a new bath or half-bath. You can call in contractors only for the specific operations you don't want to tackle yourself.

And that cuts the price by up to 60%!

PLANNING. Among all of those cans and can'ts, there is one operation we didn't include: Planning. This might be the one area in which you most need a professional.

If you are doing this step yourself you spend the money to buy the magazines, spend the time to study them and spend the time to tour the showrooms to study products and ideas. Then you try to apply them to your own bathroom.

Even after investing this time and money, it still is a good idea to consider a professional planning service.

How do you find a real pro?

First, an architect, decorator or builder does not qualify unless he or she has a department specializing in bathroom design. These professionals cannot otherwise devote their time to knowing the wide range of products available and their applications, and usually they will not want to bother with such small jobs anyway.

As suggested before, the real pro in any area usually will be a custom kitchen dealer who also specializes in bathrooms. A more general home improvement contractor might also specialize in bathrooms. Sometimes these dealers will lease the kitchen/bath department of a large department store or of a home center, and in this case it is sometimes more difficult to recognize the real pros.

But there are ways. First, they will have complete bathroom displays showing a variety of products and design ideas. Second, they will have separate salesmen and a separate manager. Third, they will not try to sell you anything without a visit to the home where they can make their own measurements and check for problems. Fourth, they will provide you with interpretive drawings of what they plan, including a floorplan and at least one perspective view.

They will be eager to refer you to satisfied customers. The best of them will accept full responsibility for the entire job, including subcontracted labor such as plumbing, tiling and electrical work.

You can explain to them at the outset that you intend to do the work yourself, with some subcontracting. They then will do the planning for a fee that might range from $100 to $500. They then will hope to sell you the products and materials you will need, and they usually are an excellent source because they will have the specified products available. Notice that this is not the same as the so-widely-advertised "free estimate." A free estimate includes none of the drawings and other specifics of a professional plan.

In case you wonder about the apparent linkage between bathroom and kitchen design, there are good reasons. A few years ago there was little more to bathroom remodeling than replacement of the three basic fixtures, and this was done by plumbing contractors. Then kitchen cabinet manufacturers started to manufacture bathroom vanity cabinets, so kitchen dealers started selling them. Then came the flood of glamorous new materials and products, such as cultured marble tops, molded fiberglass tubs and shower stalls, Corian and other decorative paneling, and the field of bathroom design came with them. Since no other trade was involved in bathroom design, since kitchen dealers handled much the same type of product and worked with the same subcontractors, and because they were professional space planners — the real key to successful bathroom remodeling — the nation's kitchen dealers became the nation's bathroom dealers.

SUBCONTRACTING. If you decide to mix some subcontracting with your own do-it-yourself activity, there are some pitfalls you should know about.

First, you will have to schedule work at the appropriate time. If, for example, you subcontract plumbing, electrical work and tile work, you will be involved with busy trades who must be scheduled days or weeks in advance. If you are doing the tear-out, you will want the plumber and electrician available promptly after tear-out for the "rough-in." The rough-in is the inside-the-wall work. It must be accomplished, and then inspected by the local authority, before you resume your work and close up the walls. Then the plumber and electrician will have to come back for the finish work, unless you choose to do this yourself. And you certainly don't want the tile man showing up before the electrician or plumber is finished. They all charge quite a bit just for showing up, and you pay for it if you are not ready for them.

So you have the problem of scheduling in advance, and then of keeping your own part of the work on schedule. If you don't, the costs will multiply.

You will get better cooperation from your subcontractors if you buy from them the products and materials with which they are involved. They often don't like to install products bought elsewhere, so what you might save by buying at a home center sale could be lost in installation. In addition, the subcontractor often has better quality available to him than you will find in price-oriented stores. But subcontractors, even very good ones, often do not have showrooms, so you must have toured enough showrooms to be able to specify the brands and models you want. Don't be unduly influenced by a price-conscious subcontractor. For your own bathroom in your own home, you should be quality-oriented, and be prepared to pay a little more. Think not in terms of lowest price, but in terms of best value for the money.

In any part of this country there will be "home handymen" who advertise their services in newspapers or in the Yellow Pages. They'll advertise no address, no showroom, only a telephone number. Many of these will be very good. Most will be good enough. But many, anywhere, will be what the trade refers to as "jacklegs" or "wood butchers." All of them will have more attractive prices for their work than regular contractors because they don't have showrooms to maintain and their other business costs are lower. If you should choose to call one of these, be sure to get references and check them, and check them with the Better Business Bureau.

In most cities, large and small, there are good wholesale distributors who maintain showrooms for these handymen and their customers. Insist that he take you to such a showroom where you can specify what you want, or, if such a showroom is in another city within a reasonable distance, ask him to refer you, to give you a note of introduction so you can tour the showroom as his customer.

Also, in any area there will be home improvement contractors who are not above suspicion. Be wary of salesmen who try to push you too fast, of salesmen who also sell siding or other things, of salesmen who don't insist on a visit to your home, and of salesmen who want you to do the measuring or who offer you a special deal if you close now. If you have any hunches or intuitive flashes, walk out and check them with the Better Business Bureau. Then get references, and *call them*.

CONTRACTING THE ENTIRE JOB. If you decide to have the entire job done by a bathroom remodeling specialist, a real pro, here is how he will work.

First, he or she will insist that you visit the showroom where products and ideas can be seen and explained. Here you will get a full discussion of the pros and cons of the different types of fixtures, cultured marble, Corian, and plastic laminate.

Second, he will want to visit your home where he can do his own measuring of the bathroom involved, check for possible problems in plumbing or wiring or check for possible design problems such as radiators or a wall offset by a chimney, and here he also will want information on family size, habits, desires, special needs. He will make an appointment then for you to come to the showroom for a presentation.

Third, at his office he will design a new bathroom for you so when you come for your appointment he can show you his recommendations with a floorplan and perspective drawings. He will offer you a contract that specifies precisely what he will do and what you will do yourself, if anything. This should include everything from initial tear-out to final clean-up. And it will include the contracted price. There is no way he can give you a realistic price until this point, if it is a real remodeling job. The contract will give you a start time and finish time, and the payment schedule. If you sign, the contractor probably will want at least 40% down, and by the time the job is finished you will have paid all but about 10 or 15%. The contractor usually has arrangements with banks or other financial institutions to help you get financing.

If you have no other bathroom in the house, he usually will provide you with a chemical toilet or arrange and plan his job so the new toilet goes in as soon as the old one goes out. Normally, everything that goes into your new bathroom will be in his hands before he starts. Nearly everything is available to him from local distributors or wholesalers. If there is special custom work to be made to order for you, he will delay the start to minimize your inconvenience with a torn-up bathroom. If your job is to include a new half-bath or powder room, he will do that first so you will have bathroom facilities available when the main bathroom is remodeled.

After completion, the designer who worked with you will visit to check it out. Ideally, he will time this visit with the last day when installers are still there, so anything wrong can be corrected on the spot.

After the contract is signed, don't expect to make any changes without paying extra. All time and materials are calculated precisely for the contract price, and if you do want a change later you should expect to sign a "change order" which might alter the final price. So think of this before you ask an expensive plumber to fix a leaky faucet in the kitchen, or an expensive electrician to fix a lamp.

ADDITIONAL NOTES. By now you may be thinking: "Who needs all that hassle? The bathroom's been good enough for the last twenty years, so it's good enough for the next twenty!" Keep in mind that we've outlined many problems in a few pages that you read in minutes, but the job itself is done step by step, one day at a time. And it is really fun to do.

What do you get out of it? It depends on whether you are doing it to make your home more livable or simply trying to improve it for resale.

If you are going to sell the house, you must think of the project in an entirely different way. In this case, your objective must be to make it look as nice as possible with the least investment. It would not be a good idea to remodel the bathroom to suit your lifestyle. The new owners will want to do that, and your own likes could inhibit the sale.

The *Realtors Review*, a publication for professionals who sell houses, recently called the bathroom one of the most over-improved rooms in the house. For sales appeal, the *Review* recommends adding a half-bath near the living area (but not one that opens into the living or dining room); or adding a separate entry for a main bathroom that opens only into the main bedroom. Otherwise, cosmetic changes are enough.

4 | Gallery of Ideas

IN THE FOLLOWING pages you will see hundreds of ideas — grandiose and modest ones; some far out, and some traditional. To use them, look at the photos both realistically and creatively.

To be realistic, you have to relate them to the space you have and, perhaps, to the money you have available. Then think of ways to alter them creatively when you want to or when you must. You may see ways to scale them down in size, or to enlarge them. Think also in terms of sub-stitution of materials. You can use real ceramic tile or real marble. But you also can get plastic laminates or even fine vinyl floor-covering that looks like tile, brick or marble, and there's no law that says you have to use floor-covering only on the floor. You can carpet a wall or a door. You can put plastic laminate on a ceiling. You can cover a wall with mirrors, or mirror your cabinet doors.

In other words, don't accept these ideas as final. Use them as thought-starters. Visualize them as they are, but also as they might be adapted to your home.

Two very different ways to treat the same bathroom area. Country styling with dark vanity (left) is enhanced by light fixtures and cathedral-arch door pattern that is repeated on cab-inet above water closet. Contemporary styling includes light vanity with matching cabinet recessed in wall, different divider between vanity and toilet, and medicine cabinet with large mirror and fluorescent lighting. All cabinets by Williams Vanity.

Extra storage space in small bathroom was gained with smaller (4'6") tub, which allows room for vertical line of "stacked" cabinets. Cultured marble top with integral lav is installed on small vanity cabinet. Cabinetry by Williams; vinyl wallcovering by Josephson.

Need a lot of bathroom storage on one small wall? This solution is by Allibert, a French line available in the U.S. but not easy to find. Firm offers a wide line of harmonious clear plastic accessories.

Mahogany with reeded front is the face material on cabinets in this luxury bath by Poggenpohl, German cabinet manufacturer. Note bank of three tall cabinets at left, the center one with a full-length mirror door. Wood lattice strips add interest to the ceiling, and towel bars are provided on angled underside of lav top.

Another arrangement by Poggenpohl shows contemporary styling typical of European cabinets. The high storage space is not practical for things you use every day, but is good for out-of-season items.

European cabinets, such as these by Poggenpohl, are expensive. But there are extra benefits in the interior accessories. Photos below show swing-out shelves available for base cabinets, and small drawers that rotate outward with a push of the finger, over lav.

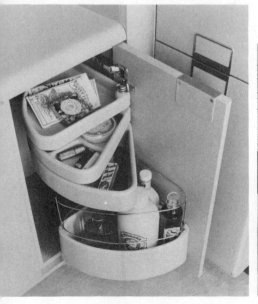

Colorful towels become part of the decor in these built-in open shelves. Masonite Royaltile plastic-surfaced paneling is used on tub, walls and cabinets, trimmed with colorful moldings that match tub.

Bamboo sets the motif for this exotic bathroom. Bamboo for bath framework and valance can usually be found at carpet outlets. It should be drilled and then nailed into place. Floor covering is Armstrong Solarian cushioned vinyl.

This is a California-style "indoor-outdoor" bathroom with window wall overlooking back patio area. Wood soaking tub is set off by matching framework and decor lattices. Floor is Armstrong Solarian.

When remodeling a bathroom, don't overlook the possibility of adding an extra vanity cabinet and lav in the bedroom. This Williams vanity with cultured marble top and lav is backed up to bathroom plumbing, saving on plumbing cost.

Mediterranean motif is created in this normal-size bathroom with Williams vanity cabinet and matching wall cabinets flanking window, and with spindles added in window. Twin lavs are integral in cultured marble top. Furred-out wainscot accommodates heater and provides shelf space. All is tied together with ceramic tile design.

Oversize whirlpool tub has sunken effect because of build-up. It is faced with plastic laminate in burl pattern. The "quarry tile" floor actually is Armstrong Coronelle.

Spacious, compartmented bath, made to look even bigger by use of mirrors, was made by combining a small dressing room with a typical 5'x7' bath. Reflected in sliding mirrored closet doors is tub wall of Renaissance Copper and Crystalline Antique ceramic tile by American Olean. This is a steeping tub, higher than usual, so there is a single step to provide better access.

Wall is furred out to provide an enclosure for tub in this bathroom, created from another room in house. Far wall is surfaced with Masonite pecky cypress paneling.

Here is a bathroom surfaced entirely with imported hand-painted tiles. These tiles are costly, but provide great versatility in design. Tiles and fixtures are by Villeroy & Boch.

Attic bathroom is created in Indian motif with wood paneled ceiling and home-made cabinetry. Tub surround is ceramic tile, extended on adjacent walls in shoulder-high wainscoting. Brown floor tile is by American Olean.

Red lav bowls in white ceramic tile vanity top are in sharp contrast to scored blue tile on wall and in tub surround. Note how course of edging cap tile "cuts through" mirror, heightening dramatic effect. Tile by American Olean.

Natural oak cabinetry by IXL provides lots of storage on one wall. To integrate cabinetry into room, space above was furred to ceiling, covered with wallboard and surfaced with vinyl wallcovering.

Sumptuous central whirlpool bath serves two separate bathrooms adjacent to it. It is made elegant with brass rods rising to ceiling, two of them serving as showers. Floor is American Olean tile.

Sunken ceramic tile tub is in its own glass room to take full advantage of outdoors beauty in this home. Tile by American Olean.

Vanity cabinets too often are considered as little more than a base for the lav. This one, by Boise Cascade, shows how storage features can be combined for extended utility, with drawer unit at left and door-drawer unit at right.

This vanity/shelf system is from the Village Oak line by Haas Cabinet Co. Shelves utilize space over back part of the counter without taking up counter space. The wood is given a five-step finish that makes it moisture resistant.

Random strips of two vivid colors against a neutral background add drama to this ceramic tile tub surround. These are 4½″ tiles that have been scored to look like mosaic, with some actually scored and cut for added variety. Tiles by American Olean.

This is a treatment you can copy in any bathroom. The rugged fieldstone wall can be real, or it can be imitated with fiberglass stone or brick. The curved tile wall in front eliminates the need for a shower curtain. Light is directed to flood the rough wall.

You can do anything with ceramic tile, as shown by this custom-built tub/shower inspired by the Japanese soaking tub. These tiles are American Olean Primitive Birch, 4"x8". Some are laid vertically, some horizontally. To do this sort of thing, you just have to build a framework of exterior-grade plywood on which to lay the tile.

"Sunken" tub by American Olean is installed at floor level, with access by steps from the shower area. Tile barrier across entry keeps water where it belongs; raised half-wall adds extra interest as well as a place to lay towel or robe.

Ceramic tile in two colors is an elegant way to "wrap" this spa-size whirlpool bath, accented by a new lighting technique developed by Tivoli. Tile is Franciscan Terra Grande.

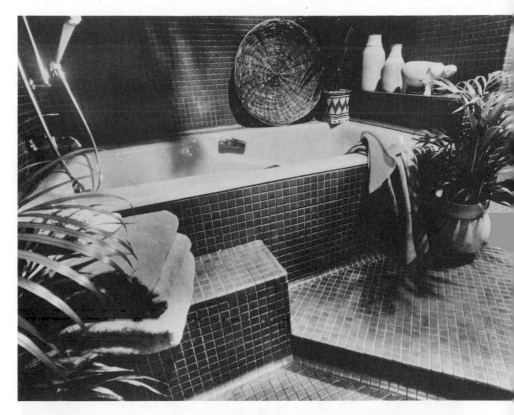

Spacious? It's only a 5′ tub. The tiles are 1″x1″ mosaics, and the combination of straight and diagonal installation makes the area look bigger than it is. Note the cove tiles that are available from American Olean to eliminate corners that would be harder to clean.

Starkly contemporary bathroom by Modern Kitchens of Syracuse (NY) features Hastings tile and fixtures. Scored-tile pattern is horizontal on one wall, vertical on the other. An elegant treatment for a small bathroom. Detail of whirlpool tub is shown below.

Perhaps you can't match the space of this bathroom, which has the dimensions of a building lobby, but the tile pattern in the flooring is an idea, as is the upswept area under the lavs. American Olean unglazed mosaic floor tiles are slip resistant, making them ideal for bath/exercise area.

"Casablanca" is the theme of this bathroom designed by Kohler, with old-style ceiling fan, rattan chair, and raised, shag-carpeted platforms for fixtures, Kohler Steeping Bath is dark brown; other fixtures are sand color, faucets are gold.

Recessed down lights in the ceiling provide an even glow in this tiled bathroom. Tile is American Olean 2"x2" bone ceramic mosaic.

This interesting sunken bath is an idea adaptable to much smaller space than you see here. There is an atrium outside, and the fabric of the drapes has been laminated and used on the walls.

No-apron design of this steeping bath by Kohler makes for easy installation. Just build the platform and it rests on its flanges on top. Steeping tub is conventional 5′ long, but it is 20″ deep, which is 6″ deeper than normal.

Dramatic sunken tub and shower area is done entirely in Franciscan Terra Grande ceramic tile, Flashed Dark pattern. Steps into tub also provide a place to sit.

Want to feel nautical? Take some ideas from this Kohler-designed bathroom with its blue fixtures and marine-type accessories. Rope ladder serves as towel bars. King-size tub is fiberglass, 6' long and 3' wide. Wallcovering simulates waves. Here again is the common technique of building up access to the tub to achieve a sunken tub effect.

You don't need a large space for a Jacuzzi—here it is in a standard-size 5' tub. This is Jacuzzi's Cara V, with three adjustable recessed whirlpool inlets.

This combination bathroom/laundry used to be a
bathroom/nursery in an old, Victorian home. The
new combination is ideal because it can service
three bedrooms on the same floor. Homeowner put
washer and dryer where shower stall used to be, to
make use of existing plumbing, and paneled entire
room with Masonite Pecky Cypress hardboard paneling, including surface of the cabinets. Design was
by G. Allen Scruggs, ASIA.

A powder room is a place to be bold and lavish, because the room is small and takes only a limited amount of decorating materials. This one has Kohler's Pompton toilet in black, and Kohler lav in antique red with Antique style faucets and mirror to go with it. Wall behind toilet is mirrored with mirror tiles, giving an illusion of more space.

Patchwork remodeling or decorating over the years tend to make an eye-sore of any bathroom. This is a small one, only 5' 10"x7'2", but here the homeowner helped it greatly with a Marlite fiberglass tub-surround kit and harmonizing Marlite Mini-Plank paneling. The ceiling was lowered and the old, small medicine cabinet was replaced with a larger one with much larger mirror. A new vanity and lav helped bring it up to date.

A wall-to-wall countertop provided a homeowner with the remodeling she wanted, with the useful addition of a drawer. There is valuable storage space going to waste under the counter, but she felt she had ample storage just outside the door and preferred the expanse of quarry tile on the floor.

Flowering plants thrive in humidity of bathroom. Since the room has no window, two grow-lights are added at ceiling. Ledge is built out from wall to provide space for plants and to help hide register below. This is ceramic tile with slate floor.

Here's an inexpensive way to rejuvenate an old bathroom. Colorful ''Tansy'' vinyl wallcovering is by J. Josephson. Wallcovering is pink, green and blue; paint is blue. Storage area is built into wall between studs.

The interesting idea here is the extension of the backsplash. Instead of extending upward only 4 or 5″, it goes up 13″, which is really enough to protect the wall. Tile then extends to the right all the way to the wall. Note how 1½ tiles are left out to provide recess for toilet paper.

Mirrors are used to face the custom cabinets that form this vanity, and hinged mirrors flank the large mirror over the lav. It all adds up to a feeling of spaciousness in a small bathroom. Storage cabinets are hidden behind the hinged mirrors.

5 | Charting the Floor Plan

IN PLANNING a new bathroom, the first step is to become familiar with basic measurements and clearances. This includes dimensions of fixtures, cabinets, and the space needed for elbows, heads, feet, and the open position of doors and drawers. These dimensional requirements must be fitted into available space.

SPACE REQUIREMENTS FOR BASIC FIXTURES. Minimum basic bathroom size, with standard tub, toilet and lav, is about 5'x7'. If you are planning the bathroom in a new home or in an addition to your home, that's the least that still will be fully convenient. In case of necessity, however, that could be shaved to 4'6"x6'.

For an added complete bathroom but substituting a shower stall for a tub, you could get by with 7'x3', but it would be tight.

A powder room with lav at one end and toilet at the other and the door between would take 6'x3', or a 4'x4' space.

While a toilet itself will be 18" to 21" wide, for elbow room you need 30" of lateral space. If you are right-handed it would be best to have 18" of space to the right of the centerline of the toilet, and 12" to the left of the centerline of the toilet. The best way is to check it with a yardstick.

A bathroom lavatory needs 30" of lateral space, 15" on either side of the lav centerline, to permit elbow room for washing hair or other tasks. It would be much more desirable to allow 36" of lateral space here.

Much smaller lavs are available, however, for tight powder rooms; some are as little as 12" front to rear. Such small ones are for occasional use only.

Standard tubs are 5' long and 30" deep (front to rear), although some models are 6" shorter or longer, and much larger tubs are available for "spa-sized" bathrooms. You can, in fact, find tubs large enough for the entire family at once, or heart-shaped tubs obviously meant for two. The big, odd shapes usually are found in fiberglass or in cultured marble models.

The "receptor" bathtub is a smaller, square model, usually somewhat more than a yard square, with a seat molded in across one corner. It is adequate for an adult, and good for bathing a baby, because it is shallower than a normal tub.

Another fixture, the bidet, is the problem child of the bathroom industry. Some Americans find it embarrassing to have one in the house, although it has long been standard in Europe. Regardless, it is far and away the best and most sanitary way to cleanse the genito-urinary area, and it also can be excellent for washing or soaking the feet and for hand laundry. It usually is placed next to the toilet. For those interested, the fixture usually is 14″ wide and 25″ deep, and for it you need 30″ to 36″ of lateral space.

Vanity cabinets are generally 31″ to 32″ high, including the top into which the lav will be recessed. If all family members are 5′10″ or taller, build up the floor under the cabinet and/or add 2x4s between the cabinet and the top to raise the lav 4″ to 6″. Any such added 2x4s under the cabinet that show can be faced with the floor-covering material. Any that show under the top can be faced with plastic laminate to match the top, or painted.

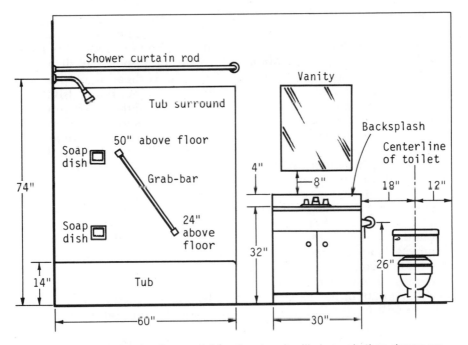

An elevation drawing is often useful in planning. It will show whether clearances allowed for basic fixtures are adequate.

If there is such a thing as a standard vanity cabinet, it will be 30″ wide and 20″ deep. But many manufacturers make vanity cabinets in several widths, usually varying from the standard 30″ in 3-inch modules, or sometimes in 6-inch modules for the basic cabinet which takes the lav.

For example, in the Chemcraft line carried by many custom kitchen dealers you will find basic vanity cabinets in widths of 24″, 30″, 36″, 42″, 48″ and 60″. Some of these will include drawers at either or both ends. Or you can get a base unit to accept the lav and add either drawer or shelf units, some with slide-out shelves, in widths of 12″, 15″ or 18″. It is a good idea to plan combinations of these units to fit your storage needs and fill the available space. This line also provides matching "filler" strips 3″, 4″ or 6″ wide to fill in between the cabinet and the wall and eliminate dirt-catching gaps.

This company also has matching wall cabinets, linen cabinets, lighting and other accessory items so you can create a fully coordinated design package in your new bathroom, something provided by only a few other vanity companies.

You should plan at least 8″ of space between the lav and up to the bottom of the medicine cabinet or mirror. The top of the medicine cabinet should be 72″ to 78″ above the floor.

In the bathing area a tub normally is 14″ high and the soap dish mounted in the wall should be 24″ above the floor. An upper soap dish would be about 50″ above the floor. If a grab bar is mounted on the wall for safety, and it should be, its lower end would be even with the lower soap dish and its upper end about even with the upper soap dish.

Usual recommendation for height of the showerhead is 66″ for men, 60″ for women. This puts the spray below the hairline. But it also means that the shower must "break through" the material of the tub-surround or shower-surround. It makes more sense to locate the shower feed-in at 74″ above the floor where it will be above the surround and not have to break through, and where it will easily spray the hair when desired. Any showerhead that cannot easily be directed below the hairline from that height should be replaced.

A toilet should be mounted in the floor with 1″ of space between the water tank and the back wall. There should be at least 18″ of knee space in front of the toilet. For maximum convenience, toilet paper should be mounted 6″ in front of the toilet seat with the roller 26″ above the floor.

Allow 27″ of towel rod space per person. To hang two towels side by side, folded, you will need an 18″ rod for face towels and a 24″ rod for bath towels. Folded bath towels need 24″ of hang space. Folded medium towels need 20″ of hang space. Folded face towels need 12″.

If you will have two lavs in the same countertop, the distance from centerline to centerline should be at least 30″, and there should be at least 6″ of space from the end of a lav to a wall for elbow room.

If you compartmentalize the bathroom, any standard built-up wall will be 6″ thick. That means that two walls to form a compartment will take a foot out of your bathroom space. But it is not necessary to build standard walls for compartmentalizing. You can use sheets of mirror, sheets of fiberglass, sheets of 3/4″ particleboard faced with plastic laminate, or even curtains.

As a final note on measurements, remember that every door and every drawer must have space to open. Your entry door might be 24″ or 30″. If a 30″ door opens into the bathroom and this creates a space problem, there's no reason why you can't reverse it to open outward, or change it to 24″. You also can consider bifold door replacements for a 30″ space if it is a master bath opening into a bedroom only, where the privacy factor might be less important. A bifold door is the type often found on closets, sliding in a track and dividing in two as it is opened. A folding door might also be adequate.

But check for space for cabinet doors and drawers also. A vanity cabinet door might be anywhere from 12″ to 30″ wide, and needs corresponding swing room, although it is suggested that you avoid wide vanity doors because the bathroom is a high-humidity room and there could be a warpage problem. In addition, if a vanity dawer unit is placed too near a wall you might find the door framing interferes with the opening of the drawers. Move it away an inch or two and add a filler to close the gap between vanity and wall.

DRAWING A PLANNING CHART. Now let's get down to planning. You have already drawn a sketch of your present bathroom in preparation for your tour of bathroom showrooms. Or perhaps you are planning an entirely new bathroom.

Now a more accurate drawing is necessary. Graph paper ruled in 1/2″ squares — available at most stationery counters — is the best thing to use for a planning chart. Each 1/2″ will represent 1′ of real space in your bathroom. One-half-inch squares are better than 1/4″ squares, because odd inches in your measurements and drawing will be more apparent.

Also with this chapter you will find a set of templates, or scale models, of representative bathroom fixtures such as tubs, lavs, toilets and showers. These are for planning purposes only, as there will be variations in size among different manufacturers. The variations will be minor, except in the large spa-type tubs where you can find all sorts of configurations. Variations in lav size and shape are found among the different brands of cultured marble as well as among the brands of plumbingware manufacturers. For typical dimensions of vanity cabinets, see p. 41.

The templates show the models of American Standard products, which are representative of the industry. In addition, two specialty items are included — Kohler's Habitat and Environment.

LAVATORIES

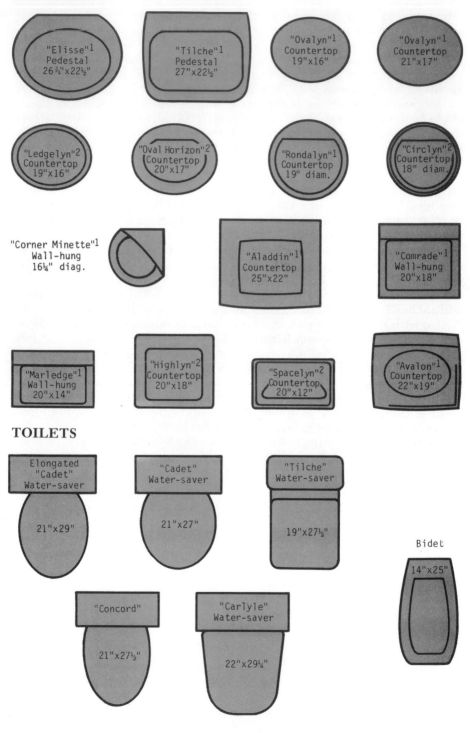

"Elisse"[1]
Pedestal
26¾"x22½"

"Tilche"[1]
Pedestal
27"x22½"

"Ovalyn"[1]
Countertop
19"x16"

"Ovalyn"[1]
Countertop
21"x17"

"Ledgelyn"[2]
Countertop
19"x16"

"Oval Horizon"[2]
Countertop
20"x17"

"Rondalyn"[1]
Countertop
19" diam.

"Circlyn"[2]
Countertop
18" diam.

"Corner Minette"[1]
Wall-hung
16¼" diag.

"Aladdin"[1]
Countertop
25"x22"

"Comrade"[1]
Wall-hung
20"x18"

"Marledge"[1]
Wall-hung
20"x14"

"Highlyn"[2]
Countertop
20"x18"

"Spacelyn"[2]
Countertop
20"x12"

"Avalon"[1]
Countertop
22"x19"

TOILETS

Elongated
"Cadet"
Water-saver

21"x29"

"Cadet"
Water-saver

21"x27"

"Tilche"
Water-saver

19"x27½"

Bidet

14"x25"

"Concord"

21"x27½"

"Carlyle"
Water-saver

22"x29¼"

44   [1] Vitreous china
       [2] Enameled cast iron

TUBS AND SHOWERS

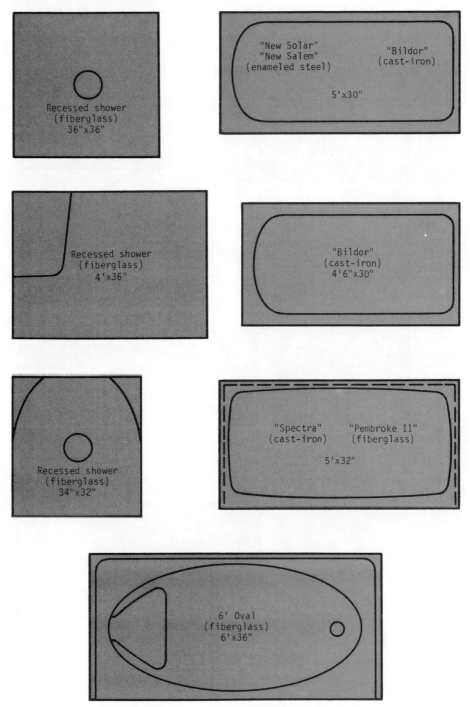

Recessed shower
(fiberglass)
36"x36"

"New Solar"
"New Salem"
(enameled steel)

"Bildor"
(cast-iron)

5'x30"

Recessed shower
(fiberglass)
4'36"

"Bildor"
(cast-iron)
4'6"x30"

Recessed shower
(fiberglass)
34"x32"

"Spectra"
(cast-iron)

"Pembroke II"
(fiberglass)

5'x32"

6' Oval
(fiberglass)
6'x36"

DESIGNER TUBS

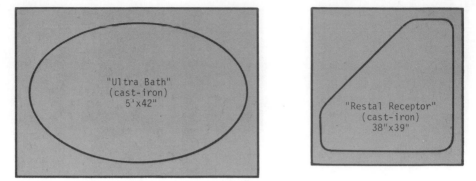

"Ultra Bath"
(cast-iron)
5'x42"

"Restal Receptor"
(cast-iron)
38"x39"

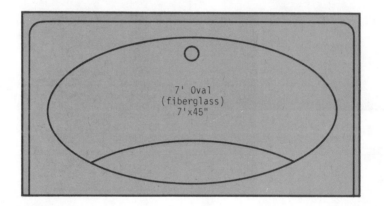

7' Oval
(fiberglass)
7'x45"

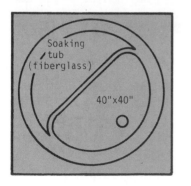

Soaking
tub
(fiberglass)

40"x40"

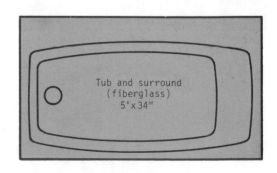

Tub and surround
(fiberglass)
5'x34"

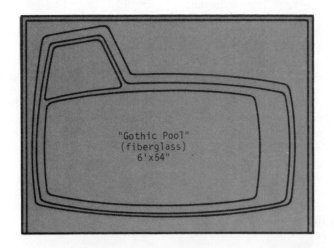

"Gothic Pool"
(fiberglass)
6'x54"

Kohler Environment
107"x44"
(recessed behind wall)

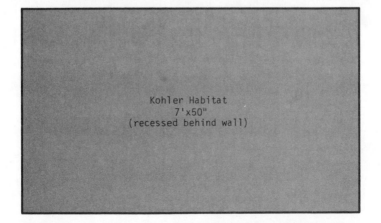

Kohler Habitat
7'x50"
(recessed behind wall)

Sample Planning Experiments. The idea now is to draw in the walls of your bathroom on your graph paper planning chart. Cut out the templates so you can move them around within the to-scale walls of your own bathroom to see what will fit, and how. This moving-around procedure will give you much more design freedom than you would get by drawing them in or by attempting to visualize.

When you get a placement, remembering elbow-room considerations, then you can draw in your new bathroom. But remember you will incur extra expense if you move plumbing lines. You can minimize the extra expense by keeping the toilet in the same place, but moving the other fixtures if needed.

Now let's try it, step by step.

1. Draw in the walls of your bathroom on the chart. Let's say it is 6' along one wall, 8' along the other, an interior room so it has no window, and with one door the way a builder usually places it. Place a big dot exactly in the locations of the three drain lines, below where the plumbing goes into the wall.

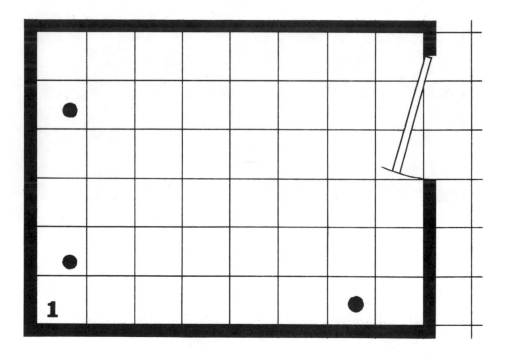

2. Now first, do it the most inexpensive way, simply replacing the old fixtures with new. You will place them over the old drain lines, but you will have a modern toilet, a modern new bathtub with an added privacy screen between tub and toilet, possibly a planter box on top of it, and a modern lav in a 24"-wide vanity cabinet.

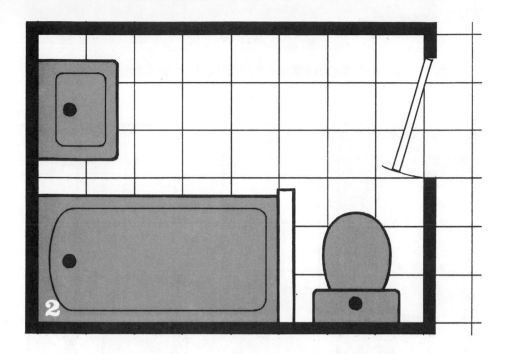

3. But wait. Move your templates around. There are other ways and, after all, you want a new look. If you move your standard 5′ tub to the short wall it still will leave good open space in the room, but will also permit addition of a linen closet at the end of the tub. That's a positive gain. You have replaced the old toilet with the new in precisely the old position because this would be the most costly item to move, but the other plumbing changes are relatively minor with either copper or plastic piping.

Shelves for linen

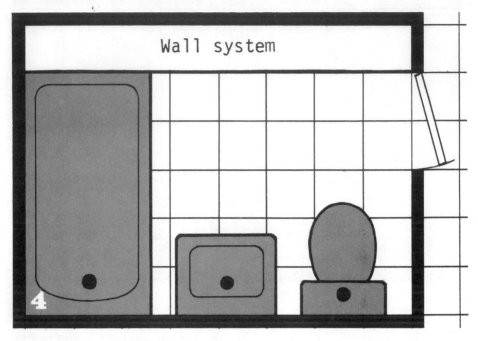

Wall system

4. But keep on looking. Notice you have a lot of space in front of the toilet and lav, and 5′ of wall space that is not used. Good space planning is the key to success in these small rooms. So instead of that linen closet — or keeping it, for that matter — why not make an entire wall system on that wall, intermixing cabinets and open shelving? This should be 12″ deep to be practical, and the only problem that arises is that the doorway opening is only 6″ from the long wall. But notice that the doorway is 30″ wide (2½ squares of your graph paper) and a 24″ door would be quite adequate for this room. You can reframe the doorway to take a 24″ door. If it swings inward, reverse it to swing outward (so its swing would not be blocked by knobs or pulls of the wall system) and you will have more room to work with.

5. In decorating, you could place a greenery box at the end of the tub with a fluorescent "grow light" above it, taking 12″ to 15″ of height, with towel shelving above. Elsewhere in the wall system mix and match cabinets and shelving for the radio, clock, storage and decorative items. These wall systems are available from better furniture stores or from custom kitchen/bath dealers. The latter can help you with the arrangement of units and also can tailor the wall system precisely to your needs.

6. Another possibility in this room is to indulge yourself in a big luxury oval tub, 6′ long and 36″ wide, which still would permit the wall system 5′ wide extending from floor to ceiling, or a fiberglass tub-and-surround unit with its molded-in seat and ledges and other conveniences. This

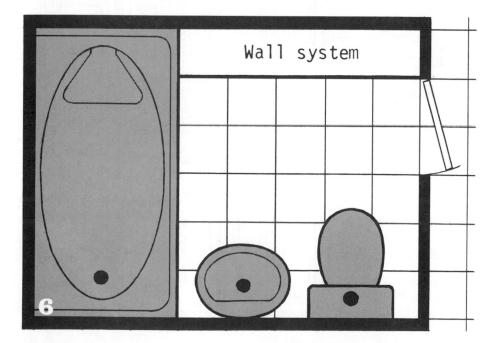

would cramp the lav-toilet space somewhat, but with the wall system for storage you would not need the vanity cabinet and could change to a nostalgic and now-fashionable pedestal lav, or a wall-hung shell lav which takes less space.

Wall Systems. You can use this same graph paper to make drawings of your wall system. These are called "elevation" drawings.

Measure the wall floor to ceiling and from one end to the other, and draw the square representing the wall just as though you were looking at the wall from the lav position. Usually the wall will be 96″ high. You already know it is 8′ long. In the lower left corner, block out the tub space. It will be 14″ to 16″ high, 30″ wide. If you don't want to use up your graph paper, use a regular typewriter onion skin, place it over the graph paper and follow the lines.

What kind of wall systems can you put on that blank wall? Here are two possibilities. Quaker Maid cabinets (shown below) are available in knock-down form, so you can assemble and install them yourself. Drawing is of the Leesport line, available in oak or cherry.

Designed by George Wolf

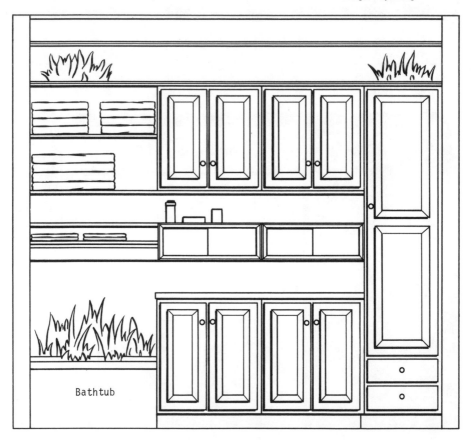

Bathtub

Design it for function and to look well. If you like to read in the bathroom, you can place a convenient shelf for magazines and books. Place towel storage handy to the tub.

But DON'T place a radio or any other electrical appliance near the tub, where you will be tempted to reach for it to change programs. Electricity and water don't mix.

You can use this same system for planning a powder room or half-bath, or to plan an entirely new bathroom in a home still to be built. If it is to be a new bath in a new home or in another room of the home you now live in, you can have more design freedom because you are not already locked in to the dimensions. That's when you have the opportunity to plan an exercise room in conjunction with the bathroom, or a housekeeping room or laundry.

Here is a system by Rutt Custom Cabinets, in Georgetown style with Gothic Wall doors. Rutt cabinets come fully assembled, but you can install them yourself. In this system, mirrors can be mounted in open areas behind cabinets.

Designed by Carolyn Hess

Bathtub

GALLERY OF SAMPLE PLANS

Robert M. Engelbrecht & Assoc. for Eljer Plumbingware

The Decorator Bath. This, in a room 7'6"x5', uses a tub and toilet made for concrete slab construction, so waste outlets are above floor level. Cost is saved by having all plumbing in one wall. Open-shelf cabinetry uses wood framing painted with alkyd enamel.

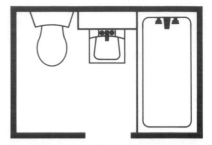

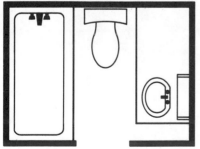

The Stylist Bath. Here's luxury in a 7'6"x5'6" room. Cabinet in ceiling has light, heat and ventilation, with added light from make-up lights around medicine cabinet. Water supply lines and lav drain run under counter to wall, for economy of single wet wall. Towel bars and paper holder are built in on vanity counter. There are two showerheads with diverter control; unusual shower curtain track goes all around tub.

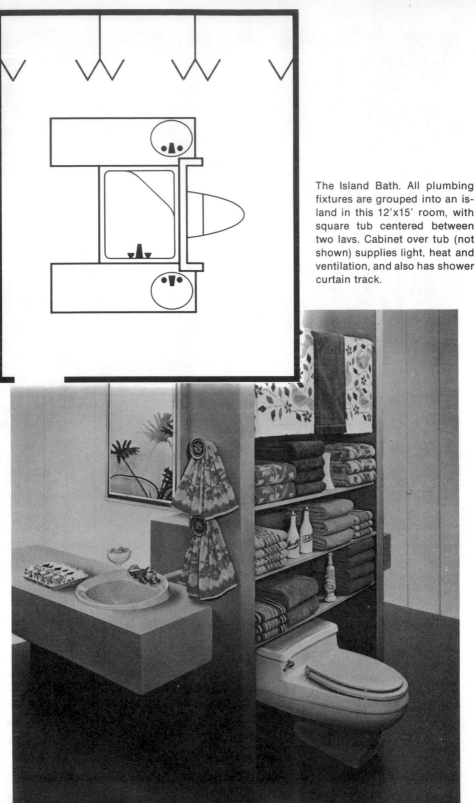

The Island Bath. All plumbing fixtures are grouped into an island in this 12'x15' room, with square tub centered between two lavs. Cabinet over tub (not shown) supplies light, heat and ventilation, and also has shower curtain track.

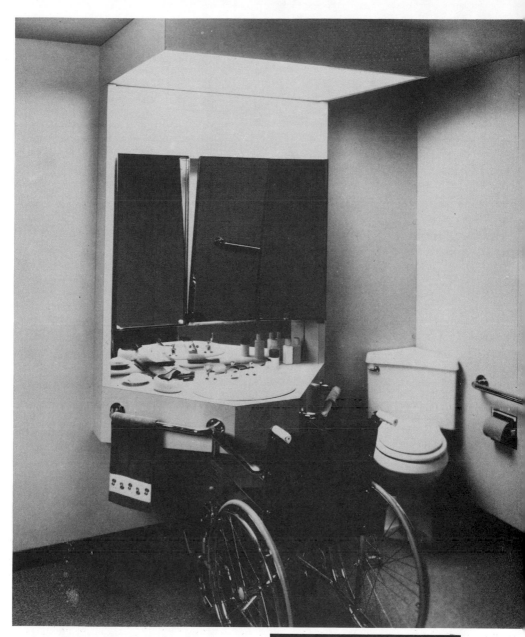

Bath for the handicapped. Those using wheelchairs or crutches will find this arrangement convenient. Cabinet and fixtures are at proper heights, and there are heavy-duty grab-bars. Medicine cabinet has three-section mirror for viewing from all angles; middle mirror tilts down. Lav faucet handles are designed for wrist action in case of arthritic hands. Dropped ceiling contains fluorescent lights. Room is 7'6"x5'.

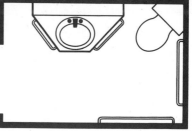

The Luxury Bath. Designed to be part of the master bedroom, this 15'x15'10" bath is compartmentalized into "his" and "her" areas with central shower and tub and toilet/bidet area. Her area (not shown) has lift-up counter section with illuminated mirror and cosmetic case. His area has wardrobe closet and dresser-drawer cabinet. Tub is semi-sunken. Unusual heat system has hot air from furnance piped into an area below sunken tub where it preheats tub, then enters the room from under tub apron.

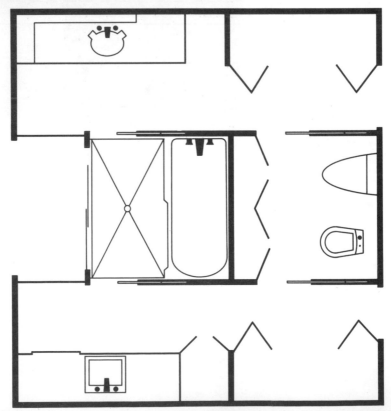

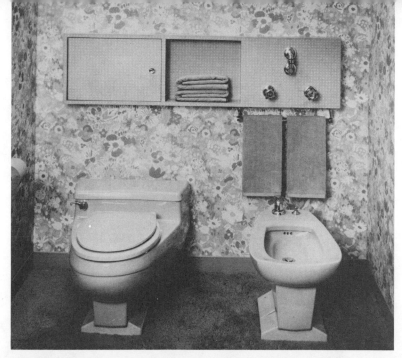

The Petite Powder Room. This 4'x4' room was designed for spare space. It could go in a closet or a corner, or between rooms, with doors on two sides for common use. This room is possible because of Eljer's exclusive Triangle toilet. Mirrored walls enlarge the room.

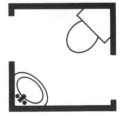

The Guest Powder Room. Good for a front hall guest bath or an alcove off the den, this 5'x5' room has wall-hung cabinetry which combines medicine cabinet, overhead lighting units, exhaust fan and vanity top with towel bars mounted on each side.

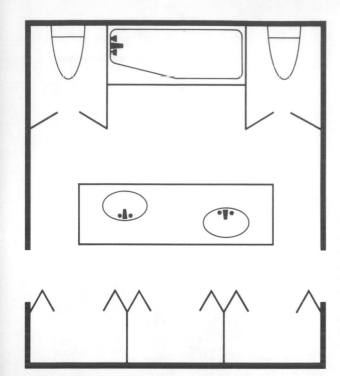

The Zoned Bath. Togetherness doesn't have to be competitive in this 12'x14' bath. Two lavs are on opposite sides of large countertop. Supporting cabinetry continues up to ceiling, holding medicine cabinet above each lav and lighting fixtures at top. Room includes a wardrobe cabinet wall (not shown).

The Dressing Room Bath. Bathroom and dressing room are combined in 8'4"x11' space. Three plumbing fixtures are in one area while an additional lav is installed in continuation of countertop, opposite a wardrobe cabinet. Separation of space is gained by frosted glass above and below vanity and a glazed-glass sliding door which can be concealed in a pocket between the end of the tub and the wardrobe. (Glass has been removed for photography.)

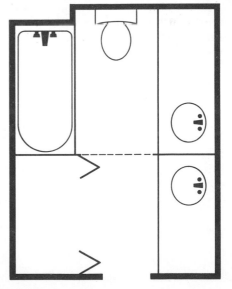

OPTIONS FOR LARGE SPACES

Sunken bathtubs. If you are working in a larger space, don't overlook the possibility of a sunken bath. Most sunken baths these days are not actually recessed into the floor. Rather, the floor is built up around them to create the effect. You can achieve the sunken effect with as little as 12″ of raised floor space on the entry side of the tub, with one or two access steps. For best effect, the steps should be as wide as the tub, and it looks better if they are deeper (front to rear) than normal steps. They can be carpeted, or made beautiful with ceramic tile, Corian or cultured marble. Cultured marble is definitely not a flooring material, but in this case it would be walked on only in bare feet. Of course, genuine marble also is an elegant possibility.

In large spaces, such sunken tubs often are islands in the middle of the room. This might be elegance to the point of opulence, but gives the maximum effect. A small or large tub can be used. But notice that nearly all tubs are fully finished to the floor on only one side, except for corner tubs with a finished side and a finished end. This is detectable in your templates by a rounded corner, which indicates the two adjacent sides that are finished. Large spa-type tubs usually come with one, two or three finished edges, in the expectation that the floor will be built up to meet them.

So the minimum space requirement for a sunken tub along the short wall of a bathroom would be 5′ (the dimension of a standard tub); 54″ vertically for the platform and one step; and 30″ tub width. With more space you can add more platform, or another shallow step, or make it an island or peninsula.

Spa facilities. If you have a lot of space available you can consider having a spa-type bathroom. Such facilities don't necessarily have to be inside the bathroom proper; they are usually in space adjacent to the bathroom.

For the ultimate in luxury you can consider the Kohler Environment. It fits into a wall, must be plumbed and wired, has sliding glass doors, and can be equipped with stereo, timers and several other extras. But mainly it gives you the effects of the four seasons in a 50-minute or 60-minute cycle. This means that by pushing a button you can get a programmed 20 minutes of sun, 20 minutes of steam and 20 minutes of rain. Sun bathing, a steam bath, or simply a shower or bath can also be separately programmed.

The Environment is 107″ wide, 44″ deep and 91″ high. The Habitat, a somewhat scaled-down version, is 86″ wide, 50″ deep and 64″ high. Kohler says the full 60-minute cycle would cost only 20¢ worth of energy at nationwide average electrical rates. The Environment would cost you about the same as a new Cadillac; the Habitat a little more than half that. But you would have an investment in the future, and probably more visiting relatives than you ever had before.

An exercise room in conjunction with the bath is more than chic. It is healthful and so it, too, is an investment in your future.

Your exercise room can be an unused bedroom or other room adjacent to the bath, but it should have direct access to the bath. Here are some common measurements for exercise equipment, although there are wide variations among manufacturers and types.

A treadmill-type jogging machine will be about 51″ long and 31″ wide. This is the type that has a frame to hang onto.

A floormat-type jogging machine will be about 26″ by 20″.

A rowing exerciser with "oars" that stick out will be about 54″ long and 42″ to 49″ wide.

A slant board will be about 72″ long and 16″ wide.

A cycle exerciser will be about 32″ by 19″ for a simple model to 44″ by 18″ for a fancier one.

A belt massager for the hips (or whatever) will be about 36″ by 18″.

A weight-lifting bench will be 48″ by 68″. The 48″ allows space for the bar that holds weights, which might be wider.

If you don't want all the features of the Environment or Habitat, sauna and steam are easy to add. A steam generator can be added quite easily to your bathtub or shower stall. You then would only have to close up the opening with sliding glass doors and furring above.

Packaged sauna units come as small as 11 sq. ft. and as large as 96 sq. ft. For the smaller solo unit, allow 40″ square for the unit. The heater and controls on the smaller units are built into the door.

Saunas and exercise equipment are not fixed in place as the bathroom fixtures are; they can be moved. Therefore it isn't necessary to plan the space as carefully as for the bathroom. Draw the dimensions of your exercise room in on the graph paper and then pencil in lightly the exercise equipment you would like. Allow room for elbow clearance.

Laundry. A laundry in the bathroom, or in the exercise room, is something else. The washer needs piping and drain, the dryer needs venting to the outside. This means it is desirable to locate the washer against a wall that already has piping that can be tapped, and the dryer should be near as possible to an outside wall or a straight run to the roof. Venting loses effectiveness with the length of the duct and with the number of turns in the duct.

The washer and dryer each should have its own separate circuit. The washer will operate on 115 volts, but the standard dryer needs a 230-volt three-wire circuit except for small portable models.

Washers and dryers will generally be about 27″ wide each, and about 25″ deep (front to back). But some are 24″ or 30″ wide, so check your own models against the space available. Compact units can be side by side or stacked one on top of the other, taking only about 24″ of floor space for both. A compact washer will wash only about 5 pounds of clothing per load. Some compact dryers are designed to exhaust inside, eliminating the need for ducting.

If you are planning a laundry area in a new or remodeled bathroom, remember that the whole objective is to make life easier or better, so don't violate the space requirements for convenient laundering.

The University of Illinois Small Homes Council recommends a total of at least 5′6″ lateral space for a washer and dryer placed side by side, and 3½′ of working space in front of the two. But if the space in front is a passageway between two rooms there should be at least 4′ of space. If the washer and dryer are located opposite and facing each other, you need at least 4′ between. For ironing, the width of the work space should be at least 5′10″ and you need at least 4′3″ in depth to accommodate the 15″ width of the board, 6″ of clearance behind it, and space for you to work. This includes space for a stool or chair.

Usually it is best to iron elsewhere when the laundry is in the bathroom. But a roomy bathroom is a good place for laundering. The National Bureau of Standards calculates that the average family uses the clothes washer eight times per week, or 416 times a year. So the more conveniently you can locate your laundry, the more steps you will save.

Consider also, though, whether its use as a laundry will deny use of the bathroom to others when it is needed. The Small Homes Council suggests that a secondary bathroom is usually better for a laundry than a primary bathroom.

Interior view of the Sun Garden window. It replaces regular window in bathroom or any other room. Available through General Aluminum distributors.

Greenery. If you like plants, you'll seldom find a more perfect place in any house for them than the bathroom. There the humidity is high, it usually is warm, and the only thing you might have to add is light.

If the bathroom has a window and you are an avid plant fan, you can take better advantage of it with a "Sun Garden" window. These are made by General Aluminum in sizes that are 3', 4', 5', or 6' wide and 3', 4' or 6' high, and protrude out from your exterior wall about 12". With that range of sizes you could quite possibly replace your present window with the new plant window, but if not, reframing the window opening is not difficult.

If your bathroom does not have an outside wall, you probably would have to add light for successful plant-growing. Several manufacturers offer light tubes specifically for plants.

Duro-Test Corp. has found in its lamp research that just about all lamps help plant growth. But its Duro-Lite brand includes a "Vita-Lite" fluorescent tube with a color temperature of 5500 Kelvin, which is the closest you can come to natural sunlight, and Duro-Test recommends these especially for African violets, amarylis, annuals, bromeliads, cacti,

Exterior view of the Sun Garden window.

fushias, geraniums, indoor flowering bulbs, lily bulbs, narcissus, orchids, succulents, tulips or any others recommended for indoors. Bromeliads would include most American tropical herbs.

Ferns are popular in bathrooms and do well in bathroom humidity. Chinese evergreen is very good and requires little care, and asparagus plants (which look like ferns) are excellent for display in hanging baskets. For color among the greenery you can use African violets, gloxinias or begonias.

Hanging baskets are popular for bathroom plants, but a common mistake is to put one hook into the ceiling and then to think it is immovable.

You can get a lot more flexibility by putting up decorative rods on two or more hooks, so that baskets can be moved the length of the rods. A network of four such rods forming a square or an X can give you many possibilities for moving plants from light to shade or simply to vary the ambience.

6 | Selecting Plumbing Fixtures

IT ISN'T AS easy to select new fixtures as in the old days. There are great new space-age materials that weren't available a dozen years ago, and the new materials allow many new design features.

The new difficulty is in matching or mixing colors. A dozen years ago or more you would be likely to choose three fixtures in matching color from the same manufacturer. Now you might choose a fiberglass tub, a vitreous china toilet and a cultured marble sink, or some other combination. Color matching of various brands is virtually impossible, so you will have to think in terms of a color scheme that will give you an integrated, harmonious package.

BATHTUBS

Cast iron. This most-durable material is covered with a surface of porcelain approximately $\frac{1}{16}''$ thick. Tubs come in a wide range of beautiful colors and will last forever if defect-free. But they are heavy. A standard 5' tub will weigh about 300 pounds, but some weigh as much as 500 pounds. Add 80 gallons of water and you add 664 more pounds, and your own weight will be a factor. So if you are thinking of an upstairs bathroom you must be sure your structure can support the weight. Cast iron also is very expensive.

Formed steel. This is a popular material because it is much lighter, less expensive and more easily installed due to its lighter weight. A formed steel tub will weigh about 100 pounds. It is surfaced with porcelain enamel, which is quite durable, and comes in a wide range of colors. It tends to be noisier than cast iron. You can ask for a sound-deadening coating for the under surface, at extra cost.

Fiberglass. This is a product of modern chemistry, made of a heavy-duty polyester reinforced with glass fibers, and surfaced with a gel coat. While we think of fiberglass as being very light, a fiberglass tub generally weighs as much as or more than a formed steel tub. With fiberglass you lose something in durability because the gel coat is not as hard as porcelain or porcelain enamel, but the good brands will last for many years if they are carefully maintained and you avoid excessive use of abrasive cleaners. The big advantage to this material is that it can be molded with soap ledges, sitting recesses and other features. Some are available with the tub surround extending up about 73" from the floor, again all in one piece.

This material is used for the really different shapes, such as the heart-shape tub for two. It comes in decorator colors. The problem with the all-one-piece tub and surround is that it often cannot be brought into a

New fiberglass tubs come with surround, some all in one piece for new construction. This, by Universal–Rundle, is shipped in one piece but can be taken apart along line 22″ above floor. Top is an optional extra.

This American Standard tub and surround is all one piece, great for new construction but difficult to get into an existing bathroom.

house, so it is more often used in new homes where it can be put in place before the doors are framed. But there are other models with surround that come in two, three or four pieces which join together easily.

In selecting a fiberglass tub, make sure you get one that has been tested for resistance to impact, fading, surface wear and stains. The major, nationally-advertised brands are dependable, but there can be cheap brands in any area that would be poor risks. Don't be afraid to take off your shoes and stand in one to test it for strength and underneath bracing.

Cultured marble. This, also, is a product of modern chemistry, made basically of polyester and marble dust cast in a mold, hence often called cast marble. It is surfaced with a gel coat. It is a material of striking beauty, available in many marbled colors, and no two items can look exactly the same. Colors can be matched, however, so you can get wall panels of the same material for tub or shower surrounds and for the vanity counter with or without integral lav. Cultured marble is heavy. It is expensive, but it looks elegant and is particularly suited for elaborate spa or sunken-tub applications.

Cultured marble bath, with matching lav in background.

Ceramic tile. Tile baths and surrounds are created by a tile contractor to fit the space you have, so the colors and patterns are limited only by the imagination and the many tiles available. It is great for wild, graphic designs and for sunken applications. It will last forever. If you should choose tile, which is quite expensive when you figure the cost of the materials and the work of the contractor, make sure you have a few extra pieces of each color, style or pattern, in the unlikely event of future breakage. The only disadvantages of tile are cost and the need to keep grout lines clean.

Wood. Wood bathtubs are nostalgia items and they are conversation pieces. They also are very expensive. They come in teak, mahogany, oak or redwood. Some have tile or other liners, some have fiberglass sheathing around the exterior of the tub part, hidden by wood overhang. A typical oval wood tub with square frame will weigh about 350 pounds and hold about 75 gallons when filled to the overflow outlet. Wood tubs should have an interior coating of polyurethane or other material impervious to water, to prevent contact between the water and the wood. Some of these come in kit form. Some are large, round soaking tubs for use indoors or outdoors, 5' or 6' in diameter and 4' deep.

EXTRA FEATURES FOR THE BATHTUB

Whirlpool units. These are available to fit on the side of the tub, converting any tub into a whirlpool bath. But this is not nearly as satisfactory as the tub with built-in jets.

The major plumbingware manufacturers have tubs with built-in jets for whirlpool action. Jacuzzi's Omni V model fits into the standard 5' recess usually provided for a tub, extends only 34" from the wall and includes a 78" high tub surround all in one piece. You buy this unit completely plumbed and wired, and it has a front access panel so it can be serviced without touching the finished walls. Jacuzzi has another unit, the Callisto, that fits into only a 4'x3' space. Both of these units are of fiberglass. Jacuzzi also has other larger and more elaborate models, some of redwood, some of cultured marble.

Steam. This feature is remarkably easy to add. We usually think of steam as something that comes from boiling water, but the water need not be that hot. Steam, simply, is supersaturated hot water vapor, and the water in your home hot water supply lines can be vaporized to become a hot, steamy mist.

There are two ways to do it, but first let's consider some structural details. About 80% of the work already is done. But you will have to close up the tub area to keep the steam contained. Some fiberglass tubs and some shower stalls come with surrounds and with a top piece that closes off the area except for the front, notably the Universal-Rundle models. All that is needed in addition is a front enclosure, such as those provided by Tub-Master. With other types of surrounds, you must be sure that all tiled areas are properly grouted and sealed so steam cannot get behind the tiles and damage walls, and any untiled area should be protected with a waterproof epoxy enamel.

One way to do it is with the addition of a small steam generator, such as those made for residential use by Steamist or ThermaSol. These are quite small and can be located away from the bathroom. ThermaSol, for example, can be up to 50' away in a closet, attic or basement, or under a sink. It measures 8"x10"x20". The Steamist model can be up to 25' away and measures 17½"x15"x4½". Either is plumbed into the nearest hot water line, and you can run ⅜" copper tubing or plastic tubing to the outlet head in the tub or shower. You will have to wire it into the house wiring, and run a wire to the timer switch in the bathroom.

A simpler way, and more inexpensive, is the Steembath by Jaclo. This does not use a steam generator; it works by atomizing the hot water from your hot water line. All you do is replace your present showerhead with the combination Steembath and hand shower, which mounts on a 20" sliding holder secured to the wall inside the tub or shower area. It can be adjusted up and down for the desired height. The unit comes with a Velcro tape which can be used to seal your shower curtain at the bottom to prevent loss of steam.

Why have a steambath? Why have a whirlpool? You'll have to decide for yourself if the claimed health benefits are for you.

Steam is claimed to be great for skin problems, asthma, arthritis, back pain, insomnia or aching muscles.

Hydrotherapy provided by whirlpool bathing dates back to the ancient Egyptians, Greeks and Romans. Hippocrates, the author of the famed doctor's oath, used hydromassage to treat the patients of his time. And we're all familiar with its use by our aching football players.

All whirlpools are not the same. In selecting one, make sure the heads and their positioning provide for full adjustability and that the system provides an even water-air mixture. And the tub should be contoured for comfort.

SHOWERS. Showerheads have become standard as an accessory above any bathtub. But it is quite common for a second or third bath to be provided with a separate shower stall and no tub. This saves space and expense, and there are many of us who always prefer a shower to a tub bath.

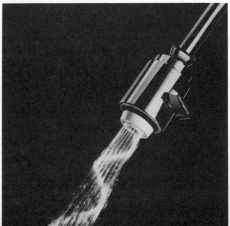

Increasingly popular in the bathroom is the pulsating showerhead with massage action. This, by Moen, has lever that flips for pulsation or adjustable regular stream. It also is available with diverter valve and accessory handheld unit with the same action.

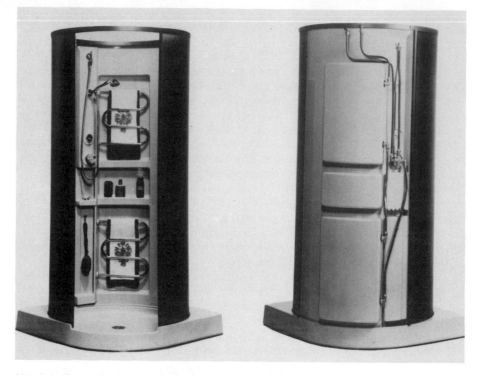

Here's a shower-in-the-round, the Aquasphere 360 by Alsons. Back panels slide open to reveal towel racks that are part of the hot water line.

A shower stall consists of a base with drain, a showerhead and the hot and cold water valves. Many showerheads have diverting valves for attachment of a hand-held shower. The walls of the shower stall might simply be the walls of the room, lined with a shower surround which might be plastic laminate, fiberglass, cultured marble, Corian or ceramic tile. Some fiberglass units come all in one piece, or in two or three pieces, some with molded seats and ledges for soaps and other toiletries.

Some of the newer ones are striking, such as the "Shower in the Round" from the Il Bagno collection of Hastings Tile or the Aquasphere 360 by Alsons. These, the former foreign and the latter domestic, have circular enclosures of translucent acrylic, molded ledges and chromed hot water piping that can be used to warm towels.

The same conformation is available from Hastings with a fiberglass tub as well as a shower base. The tub is available with whirlpool jets.

The fiberglass units are easiest to keep clean, requiring only a wipe with a damp cloth. Cultured marble, plastic laminate and Corian are almost as easy to clean. Ceramic tile is easily cleaned if the grout is fully mildew-resistant.

Installation requires setting of the base on a drain with trap, running hot and cold water lines up to the showerhead, and installation of the surround.

For the typical 36″ square shower, the drain location will be about 15″–16″ from the wall, although this will have to be checked against the specific unit you buy. For example, the Comboshower of Universal-Rundle specifies 15¾″ from the wall for drain location. This is a five-piece unit of fiberglass consisting of the base, the back, the two side walls and a covering top section which is optional. While one-piece units are available, units such as the Comboshower are especially suited for remodeling in existing homes where the unit must be brought in through existing doorways or up stairs where a one-piece unit might not fit.

The installation of other types of surrounds is described in Chapter 9.

TOILETS. Toilet bowls are made of vitreous china. Despite all of the advances of modern chemistry, no substitute has yet been developed that will withstand the acids a toilet is subjected to. However, the tank, or water closet, might be of a different material in some models.

Also, except for some imports, toilets are supplied only by the major plumbingware manufacturers. They are made in colors to match tubs and lavs, with matching seats and tanks.

Toilets generally are judged by their efficiency at removing waste, the quietness of their action, and the total water surface in the bowl which, when larger, keeps surfaces inside cleaner.

The four types of toilets, by action, are:

The washdown. This is the least expensive, the least efficient and the noisiest. But it works. It is flushed with a simple wash-out action from the rush of water in the tank. Much of the bowl is not covered by water, and it can be more subject to clogging than other types.

The reverse trap. This has siphon action, is more expensive than the washdown but the least expensive of siphon-action toilets. The rush of water when flushed creates a siphon action in the trapway, assisted by a small water jet at the trapway inlet. Siphon action pulls the waste from the bowl. More of the bowl is covered by water, so it stays cleaner.

Siphon jet. Most of the interior of the bowl is covered by water in this model and the trapway is larger. Flushing action is quieter. It is an improvement and refinement over the reverse trap, and more expensive.

Low profile. This has action basically similar to the siphon jet, but toilet and tank are all one piece and it is considered generally more elegant. There is very little dry surface in the bowl interior, and flushing action is very quiet and most efficient.

In choosing your toilet, you will see that some have rounder bowls, some more oval in shape. The latter are called "extended rim," and are usually more comfortable and easier to keep clean.

Some models are wall-hung, mounted off the floor. This makes for easy floor cleaning, and you might consider them more attractive. But installation is more expensive, because they need a special metal "chair carrier" in the wall mounted to 2x6 studs. (Normally, wall studs are 2x4s.) If you are creating a new bathroom you can use 2x6 studs on that wall and the installation cost differential might be almost insignificant.

You also can find special-shape toilets to fit into a corner, and extra-high toilets that can be better for the aged or infirm.

Remember also that toilets use a lot of water. See Appendix A on water and energy saving.

BIDETS. In Europe and South America, women reportedly used to think the bidet was a useful device for birth control.

But its use is quite general in those areas for a good and quite different reason: It is probably the most sanitary way there is for the entire family to wash the perineal area after using the toilet.

There isn't much difference between brands in bidets. They are shaped somewhat like a toilet but have no seat like that of a toilet. They are best placed alongside the toilet and, like other fixtures, they are made to match the colors of tub, toilet and lav.

Hot and cold water controls usually are mounted on the wall. The user sits on the bidet facing the controls. The bidet bowl has a pop-up stopper like a lav, to hold water in the bowl. A transfer valve produces a soothing spray directed toward the user, then diverts the spray to the rim to clean the bidet.

Some manufacturers mount the hot and cold water controls on the bidet itself, so they are right in front of the user.

The fixture also is useful for washing or soaking the feet.

LAVATORIES. Bathroom lavs come large and small, deep and shallow, in many shapes, colors and materials. Some stand on pedestals for a nostalgic touch, resembling those of decades ago. Some are like shells. Some are shaped for easy bathing of a baby. Others are tiny to fit into small powder rooms. Some are molded in as an integral part of the countertop. Some are just plain sinks.

Vitreous china still is a popular material for the lav. This is nature's own rock, so you won't find anything more lasting. Some vitreous models are made larger to occupy the entire top of a vanity cabinet, with molded-in recesses for soaps. Others must be fitted into a top such as plastic laminate or cultured marble; either fitted underneath, resting on top with a water-proofing mastic, or clamped with a metal rim. Others are wall-hung.

All of these shapes and sizes are available in porcelained cast iron, also. Or you can choose porcelain enameled steel or even stainless steel.

But probably the most popular now is the cultured marble top with integral bowl, at least in bathroom remodeling. The integral bowl eliminates the purchase and installation of a separate lav, and the lav has the same colorful veining as the countertop.

While most cultured marbles are solid, heavy combinations of molded polyester and marble dust, as previously described, there are other plastics used in lavs. Some use acrylics or ABS (acrilonitrile butadiene styrene) with a fiberglass backing for rigidity, and these can be with or without integral bowl. Corian is a form of cultured marble, but we treat it

The Elisse (left) and Tilche pedestal lavs by American Standard, with contemporary styling and larger than average basin areas. They're of vitreous china; stand 31″ and 32″ high, respectively; and come in a range of colors. Shown with Ultra Font faucets.

Sculptured pedestal lavatory of genuine marble, by Sherle Wagner.

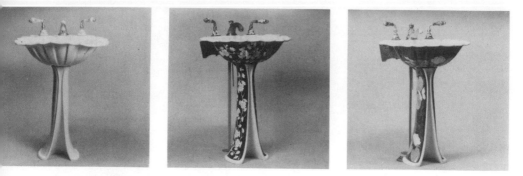

Other Sherle Wagner pedestal models, all hand-painted china with full-size bowls, but with space-saver dimensions overall. They are 18½″ front to back, 23″ across and 32″ high.

separately because of its unique workability with woodworking tools. American Standard also offers lavs made of melamine plastic, in addition to vitreous china, steel and cast iron.

The quality materials here are cast iron, vitreous china and the heavy cultured marble or Corian. The others are less expensive, lighter in weight and less elegant. The Corian top with integral bowl, or double bowl, will be most expensive unless you go to a fully tiled countertop.

In a small powder room the temptation is to go with the simple, least expensive lav. But this often is used a lot by guests, and it requires storage space also. So even when the space is only 36″ wide, you still could fit in a 36″ vanity cabinet and make it elegant with a cultured marble top with integral lav. That way, you would also save the work of installing a separate lav.

For details on installing all kinds of tops, see Chapter 8.

Two vitreous china lavs by American Standard—the Avalon (left), with Aquarian II faucet, and the Aqualady, with Heritage faucet. Countertop at right is preformed plastic laminate.

Here's something only available from a Poggenpohl dealer—a bathroom lav meticulously fused to the plastic laminate countertop so nothing shows except the edge of the laminate. Lav was inserted from underneath.

DECORATIVE FAUCETS

One of the most expensive possibilities—fittings in gold plate or brushed chrome, accompanied by hand-painted basin. From the Museum line by Sherle Wagner.

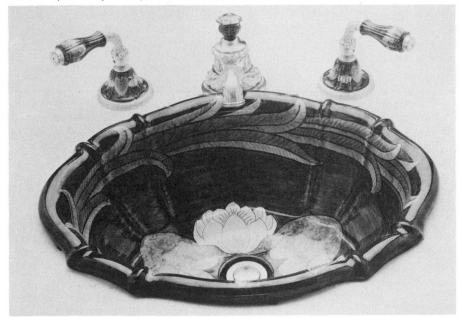

Decorative Faucets, continued

Lav faucet and tub shower valve in Silvertone Brocade finish by Moen.

Olympian style fixture by Bradley has crystal-like levers, with base in bright or brushed chrome or brushed gold.

The Aphrodite by Bradley has 24-carat gold trimming on vitreous china, with a lifetime guarantee against leaks or drips.

Geometric shapes in mirror chrome or gold finish, from Sherle Wagner's Sculpture line.

Deltique line by Delta has an ornate look, with gold-tone finish and crystal handles.

7 | Plumbing

YOUR BATHROOM FIXTURES are the necessary link between the two plumbing systems in your home. You have a supply system that brings fresh water in and distributes it to where it is needed, and a DWV (Drain-Waste-Ventilation) system that removes water after you use it.

Any work you do in the bathroom beyond cosmetic changes will involve working with these two systems. If you already have decided you will not do any of the work yourself, leaf past these pages. The basic plumbing need not affect your choice of fixtures.

But if you are undecided about what you might do yourself, read these pages realistically. Plumbing is not difficult work. It simply requires care and patience and a few specialized tools. Think as you read: "Can I do this? Do I want to do this?" If your answers are consistently "yes," you can save considerably.

HOW THE PLUMBING SYSTEM WORKS. Water enters your house under pressure, and is under this pressure as it is distributed through your house. The pressure usually is about 30 to 50 pounds per square inch. So small pipes are adequate for the water supply, ranging from an inch in diameter down to as little as 1/4". Your water supply lines to bathroom lavs and tub, and bidet if you have one, will normally be 3/8".

But the removal piping is not under pressure. Your waste water, and the waste it carries, moves by gravity flow, so this DWV piping must be larger.

DWV piping is usually 1 1/2" or 2" except when it serves a toilet. When it serves a toilet it usually is 3", sometimes 4".

The vertical pipe that carries it all away, down to its lowest level, is called a stack. Any stack that serves a toilet is a soil stack. Every house has at least one stack. Most have only one, but many have "secondary" or waste stacks that serve sinks, tubs, lavs or any other appliances not including a toilet.

Horizontal piping from any toilet to its stack, always sloped downward, is a soil pipe. Horizontal pipe from a lav or tub, not serving a toilet, is a waste pipe.

If your new toilet is in another section of the house, considerably removed from the main stack, it might be easier to make a new stack for it, running down to the basement or lowest level and up through the roof. Any stack must go up and through the roof for venting to outside air (that's the V in DWV), or you can get sewer gas in the house.

A horizontal pipe, sloping slightly downward, will be at the bottom of the system, collecting all waste from all fixtures, including toilets, and carrying them outside below ground level to the sewer. This is the build-

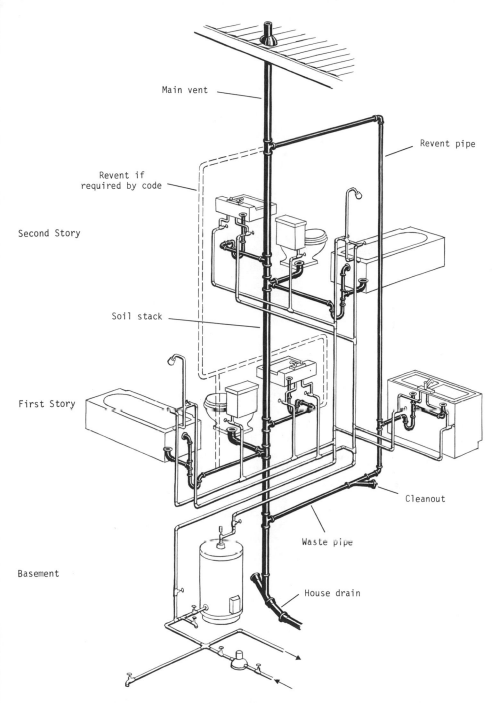

Main vent

Revent pipe

Revent if
required by code

Second Story

Soil stack

First Story

Cleanout

Waste pipe

Basement

House drain

Fresh-water and DWV systems in a typical two-story house. Note that every sink and
tub has a trap, and every trap is vented. Reventing system for first story (indicated
with broken line) would draw air from main vent to produce better drainage. In
some localities a different stack arrangement is required, so it is best to check any
plans with a local plumbing inspector before beginning work.

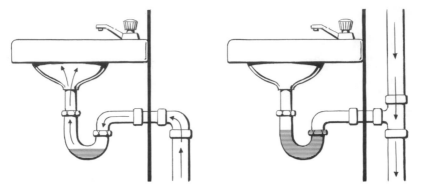

Left: Without venting, water in trap might be siphoned off, allowing sewer gases to enter. *Right:* Fresh air brought in by venting keeps water seal intact.

ing drain and 5' from the foundation it becomes the house sewer. It connects to the municipal sewer, or a private septic system.

The downward slope of soil pipes, incidentally, need not be exaggerated. A quarter-inch per running foot is enough if all the piping is properly sized.

Drainage systems must be sized according to local codes. It is possible to oversize them as well as undersize them. Soil pipes that are too large can lead to partial stoppage because they do not allow the water to flush completely the material clinging to its walls.

Venting is needed for every trap in a home water system. Traps are plumbed in at every water appliance to prevent entry of sewer gas into the home (not to give you a way to recover a ring that went down the drain as many people think). But the rush of water going down the drain system creates a siphon action that could pull the water out of the trap and leave it dry, allowing sewer gases to back up into the house. In addition, sewer gas could build up pressure that would force the water out of the trap, admitting the gas. The fresh air brought in by venting prevents either occurrence.

A fixture can be both drained and vented through the same pipe if the pipe is large enough or the run short enough. This is called wet venting. All fixtures are wet vented for a short distance, but the distance is limited by the plumbing code in your area.

If your new bathroom is some distance from the stack, you have an alternative to putting in a new stack through the roof. The alternative is called reventing, and it involves running a length of pipe upward from the fixture waste pipe and connecting it to the stack above all waste connections. It need not be the same stack into which the fixture drains. The revent pipe usually is the same size as the drain pipe for the fixture, usually 1¼" or 1½" in diameter.

In your water supply piping, it is advisable to install a shut-off valve under or behind the fixture, where it won't be visible. This permits you

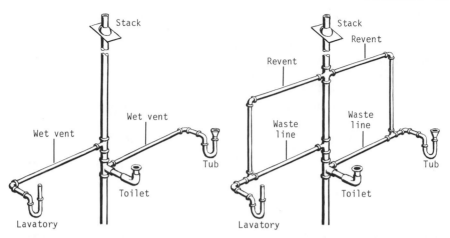

Reventing consists of vent-only pipes branching out from the main stack to take advantage of air brought in from the roof. The branch vents do not necessarily connect to the same stack that the fixtures drain into, as shown here. Vent pipes must join stack above all other waste lines.

to shut off the water so you can repair a faucet, without shutting off the entire house water supply. A fixture with both hot and cold water supply, such as a lav or tub, should have a shutoff valve on both lines.

In your DWV lines you must remember you have a gravity flow. So any waste pipes joining another waste pipe or a stack must direct the waste in the direction of flow. If you look at the stack in your own basement, where it joins the down-sloping horizontal drain pipe, you will see that it has a Y fitting that directs the flow. Behind it you also will notice a plug. The plug can be removed in the event the drain gets clogged. You will find another plug where the drain turns to leave the house.

TYPES OF PIPING. In selecting pipes for your new plumbing, you have a choice of cast iron, galvanized steel, copper tubing, PVC (polyvinyl chloride), CPVC (chlorinated PVC) or PB (polybutylene). The latter three, obviously, are plastics.

The plastics are ideal for the do-it-yourselfer. They are easy to cut, easy to handle, and it is easy to make a neat job of it. They are very smooth on the inside so there is less flow resistance, and, to a certain extent, they are self-insulating so there is less loss of heat from the hot water pipe runs and less sweating on the cold water runs. They weld together easily with a solvent and they are more durable. The only drawback is that once you weld a fitting with the solvent there is no taking it apart. You can only cut it off and start again with a new fitting.

CPVC is a tougher improvement on the older PVC, and is excellent for both hot and cold water supply and DWV. PB is good for hot and cold water supply where you want to bend around corners, thus saving a lot of work. CPVC is rigid and comes in 10′ lengths. PB comes in 25′ or 100′ coils.

Next easiest for the do-it-yourselfer is copper tubing. Some of it is rigid, some is flexible for easy handling. But you do need some special tools for working with copper, such as a tubing cutter and a flaring tool. Copper involves making "sweat" fittings with solder and a torch, always a fire hazard for the inexperienced. For the waste lines you would ask for copper drainage tube, type DWV.

Cast iron and galvanized steel are all rigid, heavy, and best left to the experienced plumber.

A possible limiting factor on use of plastic pipe might be your local code. Codes sometimes lag years behind current technology, and some forbid use of plastic pipe. If this is true in your area, apply for a variance from the code and hope they will be reasonable.

These different materials are all compatible with various fittings and adaptors. So even if you find you have cast-iron stacks, you still can use plastic or copper. However, the different manufacturers of plastic pipe make no effort to make their products compatible with those of their competitors, so stick with one brand. A recommended brand is Genova, because of its extremely wide range of fittings. If your dealer doesn't stock all of them, ask for the Genova catalog.

WORKING WITH PLASTIC PIPE

Tools. The only tools you'll need for working with plastic pipe are a pipe cutter and a can of the solvent cement used for welding the pipe. You can rent a small pipe cutter. If you also will use plastic DWV pipe, get a large pipe cutter as well.

Measuring. Use a steel tape rule or a folding carpenter's rule. Be sure to allow for the depth of the fittings that will go at each end. There will be a ridge inside each fitting, and the pipe must seat against it. Measure carefully and don't try to put fittings on in advance, because if you make a mistake there's no way to take a fitting off.

Cutting. Slip the pipe cutter over the pipe, screw the knob up so the cutting wheel is against the pipe, and make a turn around the pipe. Then turn it up a little more and make another turn, and repeat until the cut is made. You also can cut with a hacksaw or regular saw, but you must be very careful to make the cut square. Remove any burrs from the cut.

Joining. Spread a coating of the solvent onto the pipe, insert it into the fitting, make about a quarter-turn to spread the cement and seat the pipe firmly, and it is done. The key word is *Hurry*. The solvent cement fuses the two together very quickly and it then is immovable, so make sure your quarter-turn will leave the fitting or pipe in the right place exactly.

WORKING WITH COPPER TUBING

Tools. You'll need a tubing cutter, a round file, 00 steel wool for cleaning the pipe where it goes into the fitting and the inside of the fitting, a propane torch, solder and flux. Try to get compression fittings so you don't have to flare any ends. If you have some flare fittings you will need a flaring tool. However, first take the pieces down to your corner gas station. Most stations have flaring tools, and if the operator knows you he'll do it for you in a minute.

Measuring and cutting. It's the same as with plastic pipe. Be sure to file off any burrs after the cut, or use the wedge-shaped blade you might find on the tubing cutter.

Joining. Your compression fittings in tubing will simply screw together. But copper pipe will have to be "sweated," which means soldered. First use the steel wool to shine up the end of the pipe where it goes into the fitting, and do the same with the inside of the fitting. Then spread a thin coat of flux on the pipe and the inside of the fitting and place the pipe in the fitting. Twist to spread the flux evenly. Light the torch and heat the fitting evenly all around. Keep the flame moving, touching the solder to the joint occasionally so you'll know when the copper is hot enough to melt the solder. You don't want to heat the solder; just the copper. When it is hot enough, hold the solder to the joint. Here you'll get a surprise the first time, because the joint will simply "slurp" up the solder. This is capillary action, and it makes the solder flow into and all around the joint, even upwards, and the joint is made. Wipe it off so it will look neat, but don't burn yourself, wait a minute for it to cool slightly and then pour some cool water over it. Don't overheat the copper, and don't burn the house down. If you have made a mistake, you can heat the copper to melt the solder and move it, but if you do this just to turn it to put the fitting in a better position, let it slurp up a little more solder.

One other thing about sweating fittings. You can't do it if there is any water on them. It is not enough to shut off the water supply. You also have to drain it—open every faucet and flush every toilet after the main water valve is turned off.

WORKING WITH CAST-IRON PIPE. This is more difficult and requires different tools. It can be done, but here you should give more serious consideration to calling a plumber. Chances are you'll be involved with it only if you are joining into existing stacks, which often are cast iron even when the other plumbing is copper or steel, or when you are going into the main drain.

Tools. You'll need a hacksaw and a heavy hammer for making cuts, and a plumber's caulking tool. If you'll be making a lot of cuts you might need a cast-iron pipe cutter. You'll need some oakum, caulking and lead. You can rent a plumber's furnace with lead pot and ladle, but for only a little work with cast iron you can get by with a cast-iron pot or pan on your kitchen range.

Cutting and measuring. Again, in measuring, allow for the length of pipe that will be seated inside the fittings. To cut, if you're not using a cast-iron pipe cutter, first mark the cut all around, making sure it is

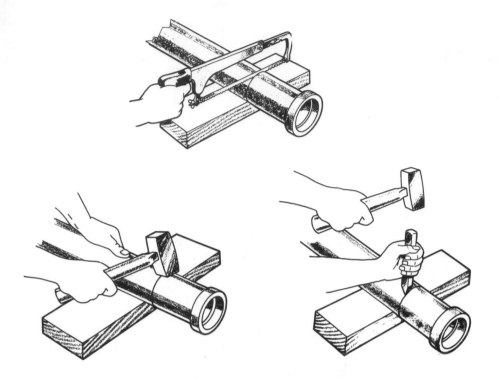

straight and square. Cut all around the mark with the hacksaw (about ¹⁄₁₆″ deep). Then rest the pipe on a piece of wood with the cut overhanging a little, and tap around the cut and just outside the cut, all around the pipe, while rotating it. Keep doing this until it breaks off. If the part that will break off is large, be sure it is supported so it won't fall on a toe, but also that there is enough space for it to fall of its own weight. If it is a very heavy grade of cast iron, you may need to use your chisel to deepen the hacksaw cut before tapping it off.

Joining. This applies either to joining two pieces of cast iron or to fitting CPVC pipe into cast iron, as when fitting a stack into the main drain. First, place the new, incoming piece into the hub, which will be facing up, and make sure everything is supported by itself so nothing will move. Then put a pound of lead in your pot for each inch of pipe diameter. For example, if you are using 4″ pipe you will need four pounds of lead. Turn on the range or the plumber's furnace to heat the lead, and heat the ladle by putting it near the heat. Never put a cold ladle into hot lead. While the lead is heating, work the oakum into strands and push it down into the hub, around the incoming piece, with the caulking tool, and pound it in tight. Do this until you have oakum packed in tightly to about an inch from the top of the hub. Your lead will be hot enough when it chars a wooden stick. If it makes the stick flame it will be too hot. When it is ready, dip out the lead and pour it into the hub, all at once, not in

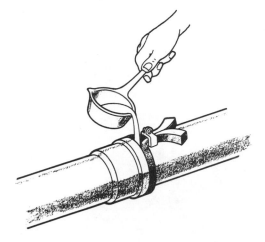

steps. Let it harden. Now, with the caulking tool and hammer, pound the lead in tight all around. Remember, lead is malleable and this will pack it in better. You should pack it in this way against the incoming pipe, then against the inside of the hub. Do it thoroughly and carefully, because this must last forever.

To join two cast-iron pipes horizontally (remembering it must slope downward 1/4″ per running foot) you also will need a joint runner, which is a piece of asbestos rope which clamps around to hold the hot lead in place until it cools. The joint runner will have an opening at the top into which you pour the hot lead. So place the piping in place, held securely so it won't move, pack with oakum as before, fasten the joint runner around the pipe tight against the hub, and pour in the lead. Then proceed as before.

The hazards of working in your home with hot lead are obvious. Again, a plumber is recommended unless you are fully experienced.

In remodeling your bathroom or installing a new one, your most likely clash with cast iron will be to join a new waste line, which might be plastic or copper, to an existing stack. This is a bit easier, because you don't have to use hot lead. But you will have to rent a cast-iron pipe cutting tool because this stack is in a wall where you can't get at it with a hacksaw. Measure carefully to calculate exactly where your new drain line must join the stack, and mark the spot on the stack. You will have to buy a TY fitting, which is like a T fitting except that it slopes into the stack more like a Y to direct the flow of waste. Measure carefully so your new TY fitting will fit perfectly the section of pipe you cut out, then cut it out with the cutter. At your building supply or plumbing store you can buy two rubber gaskets with metal clamps, called hubless fittings. Slip one of these onto each section of pipe between which your new TY fitting will go, place the TY in place, slip the rubber gaskets into place, slip the clamps over them and tighten. To tighten, some take a screwdriver, others take a special wrench.

Plastic Lead seal is often used to join plastic pipe to cast iron. When mixed with water, it expands to fill joint.

NOTES ON RUNNING PIPE. There are a few important things to remember about running pipe. It is fine if you can run it entirely between studs in the wall, or between floor or ceiling joists. But often you will have to notch that lumber to get the pipe to where you want it.

1. In notching a joist, never cut the notch in the center half of its length. Make your cut within one-fourth of the distance from the point where the joist is supported. Thus if the length of a joist between supports is 12′, your cut should be made within 3′ of one support or the other. If you notch in the center 6′ you will weaken the joist.

When you notch the joist, make sure your cut is no deeper than ¼ of the depth of the joist. Similarly, if you cut a hole through a joist instead of notching at the bottom, the diameter of the hole should be no more than ¼ of the joist depth. The hole can be made anywhere in the length, but should be centered between the top and bottom edges of the joist.

2. At your building supply store you will find rolls of steel strap with holes in it. Use this strap to hold pipes in place where needed, nailing the strap under or around pipes.

3. In running drain pipe, the diameter of the pipe limits how long it can be before it joins a stack. This is because the lowest end of your drain pipe (remember, it slopes downward) cannot be below any part of the P bend in the trap under the fixture. Otherwise it would induce siphonage and drain the trap. These critical distances are 4½′ for 1½″ diameter pipe; 5′ for 2″ diameter pipe; and 6′ for 3″ diameter pipe. (Maximum permissible pipe runs may be shorter in some locations: check your local code.)

4. In running your water supply pipe, check other house plumbing to see if it, too, slopes slightly downward. It doesn't have to, but if it does, run your new pipe with a similar slope. This makes it easy to drain the entire system from the waste valve at the low point in the supply, to prevent freezing if you close up and leave for the winter.

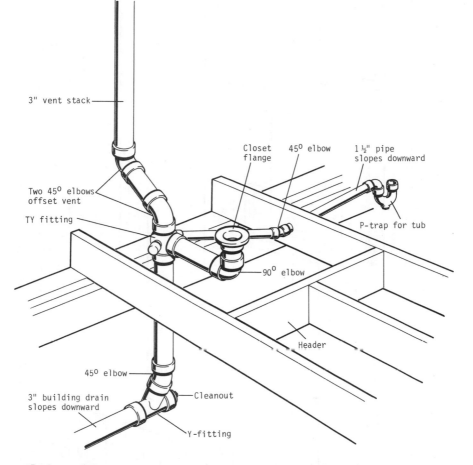

3" vent stack

Closet flange

45⁰ elbow

1½" pipe slopes downward

Two 45⁰ elbows offset vent

TY fitting

P-trap for tub

90⁰ elbow

Header

45⁰ elbow

3" building drain slopes downward

Cleanout

Y-fitting

Drainage fittings are always pitched to make drain pipe slope downwards ¼" per foot. Here, the rule about critical distances requires that the P-trap for tub be no further than 4½' from the stack. Otherwise, TY fitting would be below level of P-trap, and tub's water seal might be siphoned off.

FRAMING AND INSTALLATION. The big problem in installing a new bathroom is in where to start; what to do first. Here is a suggested procedure.

The job for each fixture is to bring hot and cold water lines to it, and then to drain away the waste. As noted before, the easiest way is to install these on a wall where you already have hot and cold water lines and a stack that you can tap into.

You will have to have a bare wall for some rough-in carpentry, so remove the old wall covering.

In your measurements, you will have to allow for the thickness of the proposed wall covering and the finished flooring. Thickness of Sheetrock

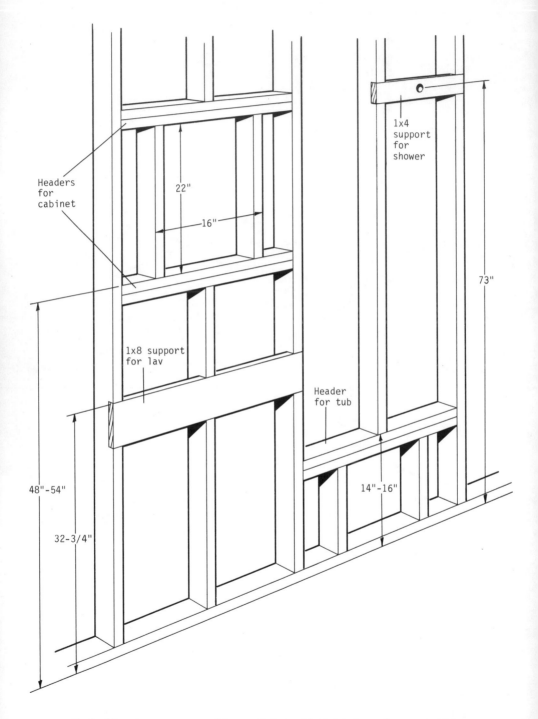

Headers
for
cabinet

22"

16"

1x4
support
for
shower

73"

1x8 support
for lav

Header
for tub

48"-54"

32-3/4"

14"-16"

Typical framing arrangement for medicine cabinet, lavatory, shower and tub.

is ½"; of plastic tile ¹/₁₆"; of ceramic tile ¼". Thickness of floor underlay is ⅝" or ½"; resilient tile ¹/₁₆"; ceramic tile ³/₁₆".

You will have to install a 1x8 board across the studs behind the lavatory. Notch it into the studs so it is flush. Distance from the unfinished floor to the top of this board is 32¾" for most fixtures, the distance from the floor to the top of the lav plus 2". If you want your lav higher or lower, vary this distance accordingly.

You will need a 1x4 board across the studs for the shower. Again, notch it in so it is flush. Place it so your shower will come to its midpoint, usually 73" above the floor.

You will need a header for the tub. For this, measure up the wall the height of your finished tub, usually 14" to 16", and saw out the center wall stud. Place two 2x4s flat, one on top of the other, between the two studs on either side and nail them in place, then restore bracing to the wall by cutting two studs to fit between the header and the base plate. The base plate is the 2x4 on which all the studs stand. These two short stud sections are nailing studs.

Now you will frame out a space for the medicine cabinet over the lav. A typical cabinet fits into a 16"x22" opening between the studs, although the overall outside size will be much bigger. Distance from floor to the bottom of the cabinet usually is 48" to 54". But it is unlikely you will want your medicine cabinet placement to be determined by the way the studs are placed, so cut out a section of stud the height of your medicine cabinet that fits in the wall, install headers top and bottom as you did for the tub, and replace vertical nailing studs for the required thickness to frame the medicine cabinet.

Now, in the floor, locate the center of the hole for the toilet drain. If you have the usual toilet that sits on the floor, the center of this hole will be 12" from the finished wall. Cut the hole slightly larger than the fitting that will go through it. The waste system will consist of a closet flange, which will rest on the finished floor under the toilet, connecting to an elbow fitting which will turn the flow toward the stack, then a straight length of soil pipe which will connect to the TY fitting in the stack.

Copper waste lines will fit inside a standard 2x4 wall. For plastic waste lines you will have to add a 1" furring strip on the 2x4s to increase the cavity to 4⅜". Cast iron will require a double-stud partition.

The bathroom lav drain will go into the wall, not in the floor. The lav will drain down through a P trap, then go into the wall, then angle downward to the stack.

Your tub will go in before the finished walls and floors. Locate the spot where the drain will be and make the hole in the floor. This also will feed into a P trap and then to the stack. If your plumbing code requires a drum trap instead of a P trap, it is the bottom hole that connects to the tub and the upper hole that connects to the stack.

Tubs. If your tub plumbing package does not have a double drain for the tub, you will have to make one with your pipe. There must be an upper drain for the overflow hole in the tub. Your hot and cold water supply lines are extended upward and joined 32" above the floor, centered over the tub, where you will install hot and cold faucets or a single-handle mixing faucet. The tub spout will be centered 22″ above the floor. The shower pipe runs up from the mixing valve, or from between the two faucets, to 73″ above the floor where it is elbowed out through the wall. You will need a wood brace near the top of the shower pipe.

Bring in the tub before the other fixtures, because you will need all the room you can get. Place it over the drain and up against the two or three walls. As soon as it is in place, protect it by taping sheets of cardboard over the entire tub, or buy a tub protector from a local plumbing supply house. Tubs damage easily from dirty shoes.

Toilets. To install a toilet, turn the bowl over on the floor on a protecting, padded surface. Fill the circular recess with a warmed wax ring, and apply a setting compound or plumber's putty around the perimeter of the bottom. Then set the bowl on the closet flange in the floor, twisting it for a good seal around the bottom, but don't lift it in any direction. The bolts fit through two holes in the base of the fixture. Secure them snugly, going back and forth from one to the other to avoid breaking the bowl. Make them as tight as you can with finger pressure. Don't use a wrench unless fixture instructions require one. Put the big washer on the threaded tank outlet and position the tank on the toilet so the holes align for the two bolts that come with it. Again, use finger pressure only to tighten the bolts. Connect the cold water line with the tank, including a stop or shut-off valve behind, where it won't show, and install the ballcock assembly according to directions that come with it. After you turn the water on, make sure the water level comes to the water line inside. If it doesn't bend the rod holding the float ball up or down to adjust the water level.

Lavs. Your lav may be wall-hung, stand on a pedestal, be installed in a countertop, or sit on a vanity cabinet.

Wall-hung models come with several different types of mounting devices which attach to the header you have installed. Just follow the directions that come with the lav. If you want more support at the front, adjustable chromed legs are available to fit from the front corners to the floor.

Usually the wall-hung lav will have a hanger strip that screws to the wall, with tabs on which you hang the lav. But some have angle braces, or brackets, that screw to the wall and then have bolts that hold the lav. The latter should always come with front legs for support. Mount your faucets and drain in the lav before fixing it to the wall, checking it for height against the location of the P trap. The P trap can be turned slightly to left or right to meet the drain from the lav.

8 | Countertops: Selection and Installation

THE COUNTERTOP in your bathroom will be to cover your vanity cabinet and hold the lav. If it is a powder room you will have only one vanity cabinet, but for a main bathroom or other secondary bathroom you should consider extending the top to wherever space allows, or even having multiple tops, with or without vanities.

Your choices are:

Plastic laminate. The tried and true material found on countertops in most kitchens, it is excellent for durability, offers a choice of hundreds of patterns and colors, and can be customized for the space and your own taste. You can make it yourself or have it made by a local fabricator, and install it yourself or have it installed. It is the least expensive.

Cultured marble. Probably the most popular choice for remodeling, it's elegant, comes in many colors, and, most important, can be purchased with integral lav or double lavs. Avoid the cheap models since the best are relatively inexpensive. They can be custom-made for you, and you can install them yourself.

Corian. Much like cultured marble, but contains more plastic and is workable with power woodworking tools. Also, it is a homogeneous material, so scratches can be wiped off with a Scotchbrite pad and nicks can be sanded off. It won't react at all to a burning cigaret. It comes as a flat sheet or with integral lav or double lav. Color range is very limited. But it is elegant and you can get accessories to match, such as towel bars, tissue holders, mirror frames, etc. It is quite expensive, but it is a superior material.

Ceramic tile. Elegant; allows great design freedom; probably the most expensive if done by a tile contractor but modern methods make it fairly easy to do yourself. Extremely durable, not difficult to repair by replacing cracked tiles, sometimes a cleaning problem with grout lines but new grouts are said to be much more dirt-resistant. It also is made easier and better for the do-it-yourselfer by American Olean's development of a new base called Wonder-Board.

CUSTOMIZING OPTIONS. In selecting your countertop material, the first consideration is whether you want an integral lav. The obvious big advantage is that you don't have to buy and install a separate lav. The disadvantage is that you deny yourself a wide choice of lavs in special shapes and sizes. Integral lavs are sold with either cultured marble or Corian countertops.

The second question is whether you want to customize your top. For example, you might want a curving front edge, or a special design of your own, or you might want a dropped section for a child's lav.

Such customizing is easiest with ceramic tile, and certain options are also possible with plastic laminate or Corian. Customizing with cultured marble is possible only through special order from a manufacturer who does custom work. But simple customizing, such as a dropped section, can be done with cultured marble by ordering two separate pieces, one for each level, with or without integral lav, and then facing the vertical piece with mirror, attaching the section of mirror to your plywood or particleboard build-down with mirror mastic.

Your color scheme won't be a factor. Tile colors are almost infinite. Cultured marble and plastic laminate colors come in a very wide range. Corian's "cameo white" goes with any color scheme, or you can get the material in gold-tone or with faint green veining.

If installation ease is a factor, integral lav slabs of cultured marble and Corian make the task almost effortless. Ceramic tile requires the most painstaking work and takes the most time. A plastic laminate top with the lav of your choice already installed is fairly easy to work with. But if you make your own plastic laminate top, then cut out for the lav and install it, you have a big job on your hands. It is easier to buy a plastic laminate top and have your supplier make the cutout for the lav. It will add less than $20 to the price, and the lav itself is easy to install.

The remaining factor to influence your choice is price. Least expensive will be plastic laminate. Cultured marble will cost 50% to 100% more for the better brands. Ceramic tile comes next, if you install it yourself, followed by Corian. But if you use a tile contractor, tile will be the most expensive.

MAKING A PLASTIC LAMINATE TOP AND LAV CUTOUT. The tools and materials you'll need are: sanding block; rough sandpaper; saw (circular or saber or hand) with fine-tooth blade; utility knife with special blades for laminates; straightedge; kraft paper; short-nap paint roller; J-roller, or small roller, or mallet and wood block; drill; paint brush (animal hair); router, or file, or Mica-Nife; $3/4''$ particleboard or plywood for substrate; sheet of $1/16''$ plastic laminate; contact cement.

You can buy plastic laminate in widths of 24", 30", 36", 48" or 60" and in lengths of 72", 84", 96", 120" or 144", and in any combinations of those. Unless you want an unusual size, the 24" width will be just right, in the length you want. You will probably have to buy a larger sheet of corestock and cut to size. Be sure to select a sheet of corestock, or substrate, that does not have any blemishes on the top surface or along one long edge, or you will have to fill these in before laminating.

1. Cut both core and laminate to size, making sure that the laminate is $1/4''$ larger than the core sheet, in both dimensions. Cut the laminate by using the utility knife and a straightedge, scoring it on the decorative surface and then raising the short end until it snaps. If you use a saber saw to cut laminate, cut with the decorative side down. If you use a handsaw, cut with decorative side up.

2. Make sure core has a perfect surface and edge, filling in with wood putty if needed. Then sand surface with rough paper for better adhesion, and make sure it is wiped absolutely clean.

3. Using paint roller, apply contact cement first to back side of laminate, then to core. (It usually dries faster on the core.) Make sure cement is spread evenly; don't make it too thick, and don't miss any spots.

4. Wait for cement to dry, until it feels only slightly tacky to the touch, or until you can touch it with the kraft paper and it doesn't stick.

5. Now, this is critical. The two surfaces must not touch each other until they are perfectly indexed, or perfectly in position, because up to 75% of the bonding strength of contact cement comes on initial contact. So place the kraft paper on the core, covering it completely, then position the laminate, checking all four corners. Then, holding it in position, lift one end and fold the paper back about 12″. Place the end back on the adhesive and press down firmly.

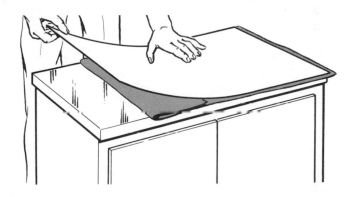

6. To complete the bond you must apply more pressure. Use the J-roller to roll with as much pressure as you can, in even strokes, rolling *toward* the bonded end. Don't roll back and forth; one roll is enough. Now lift the far end slightly to slip the paper out another 12″, and roll that part for good bond, but from now on roll only *away* from the section already bonded. This will roll out any possible air bubbles.

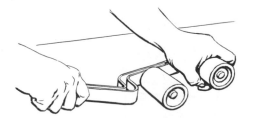

7. Now you will use a strip of the same laminate for the exposed edge of the core. This is called self-edging. Cut it to fit, apply contact cement with the animal-hair paint brush, making sure you miss no spots, and wait for it to dry. Then fit it under the slight overhang of the top laminate sheet (remember, you cut this sheet about ¼″ too big), index it carefully, and press. Use a block and mallet to complete the bond.

8. Now you must trim off the overhang. It is best done with a router. If you don't have one, the Mica-Nife is a small gadget made for this purpose. A fine file can also be used, at about a 60° angle so you don't leave a sharp edge.

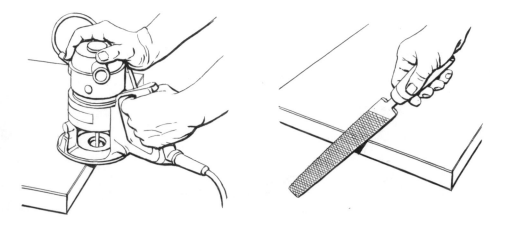

9. To make the lav cutout, check the lav carton and you should find a template you can use to mark the cut. Position it so the lav drain is in proper position to hook up with your plumbing. If your lav has no template, its instructions will at least give the cutout size. Mark it with a pencil on the laminate surface.

10. If it is a square or rectangular sink, drill pilot holes at the four corners, inside your line, and then cut with a saber saw or handsaw. If it is round or oval, one hole is sufficient. Your cut must be reasonably accurate, but it doesn't have to be perfect because it will be hidden by the sink rim.

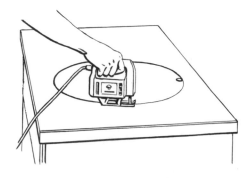

11. Install the lav, using instructions that come with it. A self-rimming sink requires only mastic. A Hudee-type rim requires a mastic and then sets with clamps.

12. Now you must cut and install a backsplash on the top, on two, three, or perhaps only one side. This is the 4″ high extension around the perimeter that keeps water away from the wall. Go back to your core material and cut the 4″ strips, making a 45° miter cut where they join.

13. Cut laminate strips to fit, and laminate the pieces on the side that will face you when installed, and any exposed edge, such as the top edge.

14. Set them in position on the top, run a pencil line along them, remove them and run a bead of caulk all along, between your pencil line and the edge.

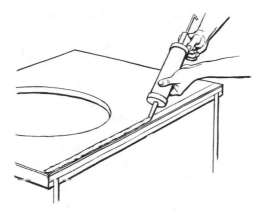

15. Set the backsplash pieces in position and clamp them with C-clamps tightly. Then drive in flat-head screws, through the top and up into the backsplash pieces, at either end of each piece and about every 18″ in between. Use 2½″ screws.

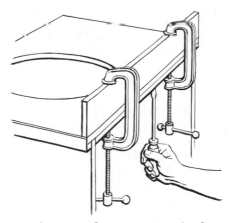

Your top is now complete, ready to receive the lavatory.

A FEW NOTES. Professional fabricators always apply the self-edge strips first, before the top panel. We reversed this order only because the inexperienced might leave an edge high and thus ruin the bond of the top. Our way is a little safer, but the other way is preferred.

If you miss a spot with the cement on the top, a "bubble" will result. If this happens lay a sheet of newspaper over the bubble and iron it with a household iron. If the paper scorches, get a new sheet and turn the iron heat down to a lower setting. Be sure to do this or you can scorch the laminate and ruin the whole job.

These instructions assume you will simply cover a vanity cabinet with your top. The top will be screwed down from underneath, so it won't warp. But if the top will extend beyond the vanity to a far wall, the extension can warp. To avoid this, attach 1x2 strips of lumber to the wall on which the top will rest, and screw it down from underneath. Four screws at the far end should be sufficient. Professionals also would apply a "backer" sheet to the underside of the core, which would balance the construction by preventing any intrusion of humidity on that side. A backer sheet is similar to the decorative sheet in construction, but has no decorative surface.

There are other plastic laminates that are much easier to apply. The foregoing instructions are for high-pressure plastic laminate, $\frac{1}{16}''$ thick, the recommended material for horizontal surfaces. But if your vanity top will not get hard wear, a lesser plastic laminate can do very well.

One such is Fresh-Face, by the Edgemate division of Westvaco. It is a semi-rigid material that you buy in a roll, in many woodgrain patterns or colors. It comes with a hotmelt adhesive on the back and all you have to do is cut it to size, iron it on with a household iron (which activates the adhesive), roll it with a rolling pin to finish the bonding, and trim. Full instructions are found in the package.

INSTALLING A CORIAN VANITY TOP. Integral bowl tops are available either $19\frac{1}{2}''$ or $22''$ deep. There are seven widths, from $25''$ to $43''$ wide, with the lav bowl centered, and five more widths from $49''$ to $102''$ wide with the lav $15''$ from either the right or left edge, except for the $102''$ width.

Double bowl models are all $22''$ deep. The $49''$ width has $12\frac{1}{2}''$ from the center of each drain to the edge. The $61''$ width has $15\frac{1}{2}''$ from the center of each drain to the edge. The $73''$ width has $18\frac{1}{2}''$ from the center of each drain to the edge, and the $102''$ width has $27''$ from the center of each drain to the edge.

Corian also offers a banjo style, which is $22''$ deep at the lav but which then recesses to form a ledge. This is $61''$ wide, available with the ledge either to the left or right, with $12\frac{1}{2}''$ from the drain center to the edge.

All come with separate backsplash and caulk, and they come undrilled for faucet holes but with a template for marking hole locations for either $4''$ or $8''$ center-set faucets. Holes can be made with spade bits, twist drills or hole saws.

1. Buy the vanity top to fit the vanity, and set it on top to make a trial fit. If it does not seat properly, you can shave the dry wall or the supports in the vanity.

2. Remove the top, turn it over and lay it on a towel for protection, and use the template provided to drill holes for faucets. Centers of the holes should be $2\frac{5}{8}''$ from the back edge. There will be three holes. For $4''$ center set, make holes $1\frac{1}{8}''$ diameter, $2''$ from center to center. For $8''$ center set, make holes $1\frac{1}{4}''$ diameter, $4''$ from center to center.

3. Lay short beads of mastic around vanity support (the top of the vanity) on all four sides.

Short beads of mastic on all four sides

Continuous bead of mastic here

4. Set the vanity top in place on the vanity, pressing down to seat it and spread mastic.

5. Lay a continuous bead of mastic along the back of the top, where the backsplash will sit, and set backsplash in place, pressing down to spread mastic and seat the backsplash solidly. The mastic will form a permanent water seal. Don't adhere the backsplash to the wall.

6. Wipe off excess mastic immediately, with a damp cloth. The mastic sets up quickly and becomes very difficult to remove.

7. Connect water supply and drain fittings, and it's done.

CULTURED MARBLE TOPS. These are even easier to install than Corian tops, because they come with the backsplash already in place as part of the top and the faucet holes are already there.

1. Set the top on the vanity to check that it seats properly. If it doesn't, shave supports so it will.

2. Remove top, lay beads of caulk along support on all four sides, set top on vanity cabinet and press to seat it.

3. Hook up the water and drain.

There are many manufacturers of cultured marble tops, so there are many depths and widths. As an example, one of the leading manufacturers, Molded Marble Products, has eleven standard widths from $19''$ to $61''$ wide in $6''$ modules, and $73''$, $84''$ and $96''$, and all of these either $17''$, $19''$ or $22''$ deep. But then there is a list of options. You can get non-standard widths, angles, notches, radius corners, different types of backsplashes, extra lavs, off-center lav positions, and many others.

LAYING A CERAMIC TILE TOP. If you have an old plastic laminate top that is in good shape, you can lay ceramic tile directly on it.

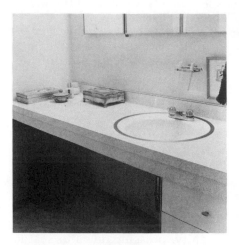

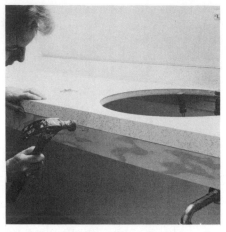

This laminate top is sound and a good base for tile. Note that the deck of the top extends ¼″ beyond apron.

Remove the rim of the lav, and the lav. Nail a strip of ¼″ plywood over apron to make it one plane.

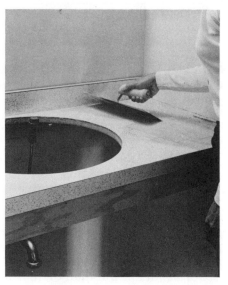

Loose-lay the tiles to find arrangement with best visual effect and requiring least number of cuts. Cuts should be made on tiles at rear of countertop.

Spread adhesive with notched trowel over small area at a time, so it won't dry before you get to it.

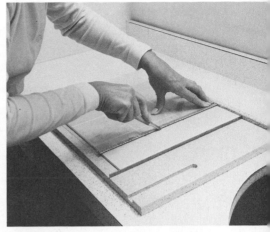

Apply tile with ¼" overlap over front of counter, and with glazed edge at front where it will overlap. This is American Olean's Redi-Set, which comes in pre-grouted sheets.

To cut tiles for rear, measure and mark tile with pencil line, then score with carbide-tipped scoring tool or glass cutter. It is easier with this plastic template which you might be able to rent from tile supplier.

For lav cutout, place sheet of tiles in position and trace cutout on under side of tile. Then cut along marked edge with tile nippers or pliers, small pieces at a time. Cut ⅛" beyond pencil line to allow space for installation of lav rim.

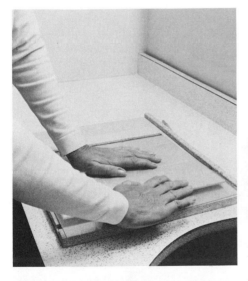

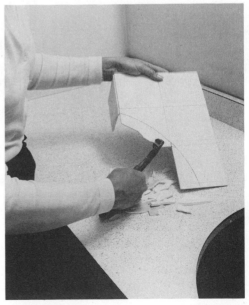

After scoring through glaze, place tile over pencil along scored line and press down to break. This template has a raised metal ridge for the purpose.

Laying a Ceramic Tile Top

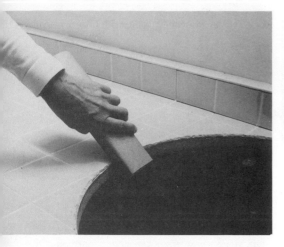

Wrap rough sandpaper around block and sand away the sharp edges. Here we have installed backsplash tiles and top caps. The top caps often can be the excess parts of other tiles you have scored.

Grout joints between tile sheets with silicone rubber, holding gun at about 60° angle. You get better penetration by pushing, rather than pulling.

Clean off excess silicone rubber grout with denatured alcohol. Wipe along the joint, not across it.

Spray grouted lines lightly with denatured alcohol. Of course, use this in ventilated room and avoid flame. Then shape the joints with a finger, wiping the finger often to avoid smearing.

And there's the finished job. Tiles along front apron go under the ¼" overhang you left with top tiles.

MAKING A CERAMIC TILE TOP. The old way, common on the West Coast where tile is very popular, often is referred to as the "mud" method. Metal lath is nailed over wooden strips, perforated metal strip is attached along the edge, and mortar then is spread to a depth of approximately one inch. The tile then is set in dry-set mortar.

The newer, easier way for the do-it-yourselfer is with Wonder-Board, a backer board of concrete and glass fiber that is not affected by moisture, water and steam. It is ½" thick.

1. Buy a sheet of ¾" plywood or particleboard for the base, make the sink cutout, cut the base to fit the vanity and the space.

2. Cut the Wonder-Board backer to fit the base. To cut the backer, score the top surface with a utility knife, break it on the scored line and then cut through the fiberglass mesh on the reverse side.

3. Lay the backer on two 2x4s for support, lay the base on top of it, index it, clamp it in place with two C-clamps, and use a saber saw to duplicate the sink cutout in the backer, using the base as a template.

4. Nail the base to the vanity supports.

5. Nail the backer to the base, using 1¼" galvanized nails.

6. For the normal vanity top you will be working with a single sheet of backer. But if you have an extended top with joints, apply a thin coat of latex portland cement mortar over joints and corners, and embed 2" wide coated fiberglass tape in mortar.

7. Spread pre-sanded dry-set or latex portland cement mortar on the surface with a notched trowel. For small tiles, use a $\frac{1}{4}"x\frac{1}{4}"x\frac{1}{4}"$ trowel. For larger tiles use a $\frac{3}{8}"x\frac{1}{4}"x\frac{1}{4}"$ trowel.

8. Set tile in the mortar. Tile is made with little spacer tabs which allow space for the grout. Use tile nippers to cut tile around lav cutout. This also can be done with a wet saw, which can be rented. Cut faucet holes with tile nippers.

9. Finish off with rounded trim tiles at edges, and with rounded cove tiles leading up to backsplash. Backsplash tiles usually are adhered to the wall. If there is any fear of the house settling, with consequent cracking of the grout line where the counter joins the backsplash, you can use a separate backsplash by attaching a 4" high piece of Wonder-Board to the back of the counter and applying backsplash tile to it, so it is separate from the wall.

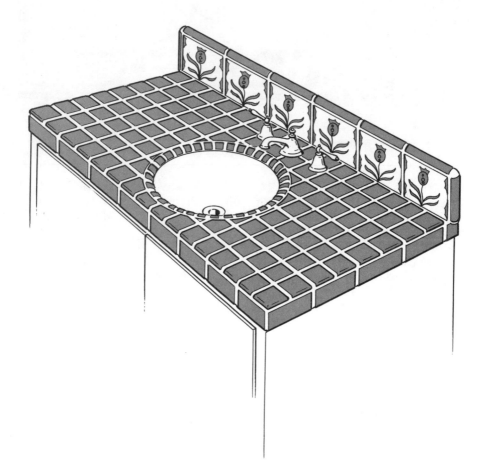

Installing tile in mortar is more difficult to do than a standard thin-set installation, but many people like the "California" look that results. Here, quarter-round tiles cut into small pieces are used to frame the lav, and imported hand-painted tiles are used for the backsplash.

9 | Walls

BATHROOM WALLS are different from the walls of other rooms in the house. In other rooms you can simply paint or paper. But in the bathroom you must consider the walls above and around the tub or shower, the tub or shower "surround," and use materials that are suitable for high-humidity conditions. For the same reason, you may also need a different wall treatment for the backsplash area behind the lav.

Fortunately, there is no shortage of materials to choose from. If you like the look of ceramic tile on the floor, you might want a tile wainscoting and/or tub surround to match. Corian is also an elegant and practical material for the tub surround and other walls. Installation of the Corian tub surround kit is described in this chapter. For other walls, Corian sheets can also be purchased separately in several sizes, in thicknesses of ¼", ½", or ¾". Cultured marble, similar in appearance to Corian, is available in panels for use in tub surrounds, but is somewhat more difficult to work with.

Plastic laminate is packaged in kit form for a tub surround, with special corner moldings that prevent moisture leakage. Several manufacturers including Masonite and Marlite also produce paneling in simulated wood and other designs for bathroom applications, treated with plastic to withstand humid conditions. Finally, if your bathroom will be a new addition to the house, or if you are thinking of replacing an existing tub, you can consider a fiberglass (or ABS or acrylic) tub and surround.

TILE. Generally, the four kinds of tile are:

Glazed wall tile. This has the largest range of colors, designs and glazes, and there is a heavy-duty glaze that is suitable for floors. Usual sizes used for walls are 4½"x4½" or 6"x6".

Ceramic mosaic tile. This is tile, glazed or unglazed, with a face area of less than 6 square inches. These small tiles usually are sold mounted on paper-backed or mesh-backed sheets for easier installation. Unglazed mosaics come in earth colors, but glazed tiles come in all colors and patterns, or you can order custom color combinations.

Quarry tile. This usually is used for floors, but can be used on walls. It comes glazed or unglazed, in squares ranging from 4" to 9". The familiar unglazed color is earthen red, but there are also sand, caramel and blue colors. Glazed tile comes in all colors.

Pavers. For flooring, but usable for walls. It is similar to mosaic in composition, but thicker and larger.

Some tile companies sell tile in packages, and provide charts telling how many tiles you need for given areas, how much adhesive and how much grout.

Generally, one pint of grout will take care of up to 30 square feet, and you will need one quart of adhesive for each 13 square feet. Read the labels of adhesive containers to find one that is compatible with the surface you are covering.

While you don't want to overbuy, always allow a few extra tiles for breakage and for practice in cutting and nipping.

You can tile over almost any surface that is structurally sound, dry, clean and level. But loose and damaged plaster, wallpaper and paint should be removed before tiling. Newly plastered walls should be sealed and glossy or painted surfaces should be sanded.

In tiling, you should start in the middle of the area and work outward. Use a plumb line or level to draw horizontal and vertical lines on the wall, establishing the center, then lay out a course of loose tile to the left or right. Then adjust the center line left or right so you get the least number of cuts. Your cuts at either the left or right limits should never be less than half a tile.

In tiling a tub surround you need a waterproof base under the tile. Draw the horizontal line a full tile above the low point of the tub edge. If the tub is not exactly level, don't set the tiles to follow the tub line. Keep the tile lines level.

Left
out angle

Right
out angle

Tub
edging

Edging caps

Cove base

Some of the trim tiles for corners and edges available from American Olean. Trim to match mosaic and scored type tiles is also available.

If you are installing wallboard, don't butt it against the edge of the tub. Allow ¼″ space between the edge of the tub and the wallboard. Install the first course of tile a little below that, ⅛″ above the tub. You will fill that gap with caulking later. Note that there are special tiles with rounded edges for corners, and there are base tiles and edging caps.

To determine how many tiles you need, calculate the area to be covered in square feet. Calculate each wall separately. Multiply the overall width by the height of the wall to get the square feet. Then subtract the square footage of any window, door or other area that won't be tiled.

Multiply the total square feet to be covered by the number of tiles you can put in one square foot. If you are using regular wall tiles in 4″x4″, 4¼″x4¼″ or 4½″x4½″ sizes, estimate nine tiles per square foot. With 6″x6″ tiles, there will be four tiles per square foot.

But some of those will be corner tiles; the bottom row, or course, will be base tiles; and the top course will be edge tiles. Count the number of each, and make a list of the number of each type you will need.

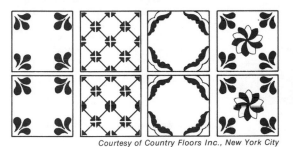

Hand-painted tiles imported from Holland, Italy, Mexico, Spain and other countries are available from distributors in many parts of the country. They come in a great range of colors and patterns, but are sometimes irregular in shape and thus more difficult to install than factory-made tiles.

Courtesy of Country Floors Inc., New York City

INSTALLING A CERAMIC TILE TUB SURROUND. This step-by-step procedure applies to any wall installation of ceramic tile. You can use the same procedure for wainscoting, backsplash or the entire bathroom. We illustrate the tub surround because it is complicated by the plumbing connections.

Tools. For laying tile, you'll need a straightedge, tape rule, chalk line, square, tile cutter, notched trowel, rubber trowel, and tile nipper. If you are installing wallboard, you will need a scoring tool, hammer, screwdriver, and electric drill with hole-cutter attachment.

Materials. You will need the tile, and here you should consult with an expert at the store. Some tiles come in pre-grouted sheets, some with adhesive on the back, some with built-in spacers to allow for even grout lines. (You can also buy spacers separately.) Use the grout recommended by the tile manufacturer, and an adhesive compatible with the surface you are covering.

Photo sequence on installing ceramic tile begins on page 110.

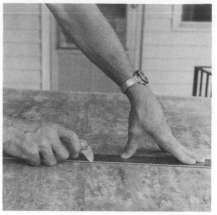

Remove old surround. Here, old plastic tile was chipped off with screwdriver and putty knife.

Walls must have a moisture-proof base for the tile. You can use an exterior-grade plywood. But the best material for it is American Olean's Wonder-Board, made of lightweight concrete and fiberglass. Score the Wonder-Board with a scoring tool, cutting through the top layer of fiberglass to the concrete core.

Cut through fiberglass on other side.

Place a board or horses under the scored line and press down on each side to break.

Measure for pipe holes, and mark positions on Wonder-Board.

Using a hammer and screwdriver, cut pipe holes. If you are a good hammer-wielder, you can make the pipe holes with a hammer alone. But the screwdriver method is more accurate.

Trim pipe holes with utility knife.

Check fit of board over pipe holes, and nail Wonder-Board in position over studs. Don't worry about the old finish, or old mastic on walls, except for large build-ups that can be filed smooth easily.

Here is the completed Wonder-Board installation. Note that it is not needed outside the tub alcove, where you can apply tile directly to the wallboard.

Cut fiberglass tape, which comes with Wonder-Board, for use over seams and corners. Tape corners and all seams, securing tape with dry-set mortar. Mortar need be only thick enough to embed tape.

Here is your completed Wonder-Board installation with seams and corners taped. Up high, out of the water splash area, tape is not needed.

Apply dry-set mortar over Wonder-Board, using a notched trowel at a 45° angle. It saves a lot of work to use American Olean's pre-grouted Redi-Set system, shown here, which enables you to install 16 tiles at a time and grout only around the perimeter.

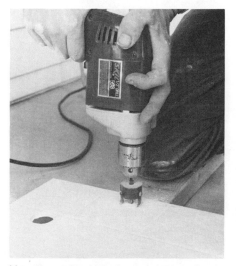

Measure and mark holes for pipes and cut with a hole cutter attached to your electric drill.

Check to make sure holes are in the right places, then continue installation.

Inserts. But wait. Perhaps you would like a few bits of color in the wall. You can do it easily, using Redi-Set in another color, or perhaps even a decorative designer tile. Lay the insert tile over the regular wall tile, mark around it. Then use a straightedge or triangle and score heavily with a glass cutter. Be sure to allow an extra ⅛″ all around for grout. Score on the glazed side, and break the tiles evenly by placing a pencil under the score and pressing down on both sides. Trim with a file if necessary for an even line.

Put up your pre-cut sheet, then install the insert.

For the soap dish, cut out two of the Redi-Set tiles along the silicone grout lines. Punch several holes in the Wonder-Board with a hammer and screwdriver for a better glue bond.

Apply silicone adhesive liberally for soap dish, and press it into place. There will be space around it for grout.

Grout all joints between sheets and around soap dish with same silicone rubber used in sheets.

Before tiling the remainder of the wall, make sure these surfaces are firm and clean. And here is your finished job.

TILING THE OTHER WALLS. While Wonder-Board is excellent for walls exposed to water or other walls that do not provide a firm support, a gypsum board wall that is smooth and clean can be tiled over directly.

To tile a wall above the baseboard, measure up one tile, adding ¼" for the grout line at the bottom, and draw a horizontal line at the level of the lowest point. Tack a board to the wall along this line as a temporary base for the first course, and check it with a level. Tiling starts above the bottom course because tiles in the bottom course may have to be cut to maintain the level.

Use a plumb bob to chart a straight line between the temporary base and a point high on the wall to help maintain verticality. Then loose-lay a course to make sure you do not end up with less than half a tile at either end of the course, and mark the center from which you will start.

Trowel on the adhesive a few square feet at a time, holding the notched trowel at a 45° angle.

Press tiles into the adhesive with a slight twisting motion and push firmly into place, making sure the built-in spacers butt against each other for uniform grout lines.

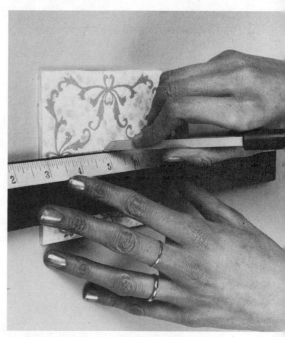

For the space above the lav, follow the same procedure as before to install a temporary baseboard. Tiles around the lav will have to be cut with tile nippers where they fit around corners.

Straight cuts can be made easily. Use a scoring tool and a straightedge to score through the glaze. Then put a pencil or match sticks under the scored line and press down firmly to break tile.

Tiling Other Walls

Grout is "washed" over the surface. Be sure it is pressed down to fill the spaces between tiles.

At a place like this window, you have to decide whether to have the face tile overlap the edges of the window tile or, as here, the reverse. Some tile patterns have rounded trim pieces for such applications as this.

INSTALLING A CORIAN TUB SURROUND. Corian is a practical material for the tub surround or other walls. Its surface is non-porous and the material is homogeneous, so color and pattern go all the way through. It is one of the most easily cleaned materials, and is easy to install because it can be cut with power woodworking tools.

Above grade, Corian should never be installed directly to concrete, cinderblock or masonry walls. These types of walls should first be studded out with 2x4s covered with gypsum board or, as many kitchen/bath specialists prefer, Wonder-Board. Below grade, Corian should not be used on exterior masonry walls, even with studding and moisture barrier.

Power tools you will need include an electric drill with drill bits; a saber saw with metal-cutting blade, 12–14 teeth per inch; a belt sander with 50 to 80 grit paper. Other tools needed are: a caulking gun, file, scribe or pencil compass, square, level, tape measure, hammer, nails, shims. Clean-up materials include masking tape, putty knife or caulk remover tool, alcohol (such as shellac thinner), cheesecloth. You will also need a tub protector, two sawhorses and three 8–foot 2x4s to support the Corian sheet.

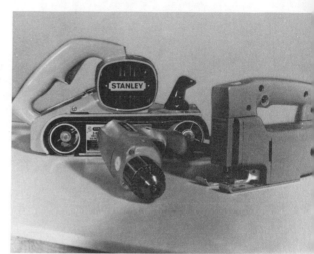

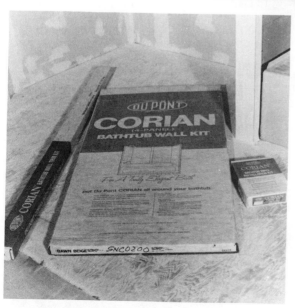

Materials will be one Corian Bathtub Wall Kit, consisting of four precut ¼" sheets, 29 5/16"x57", and one ¼" batten strip 6"x57"; one Corian Trim Kit consisting of four pieces of ½" Corian, 2"x74"; and a Corian Installation Kit consisting of three tubes of neoprene panel adhesive for bonding panels to the wall, and one tube of silicone sealant for waterproof caulking of joints, battens and trim strips.

Set up the sawhorses with two of the 2x4 rails to support the Corian sheet and the third rail to provide support for the underside of the sheet in the spot being drilled or cut.

Cover tub with the tub protector to protect it from scratches. Check that there is ½" space between the wallboard and the tub flange. If not, make the space with a utility knife. This prevents water from wicking up the wallboard should a leak ever develop.

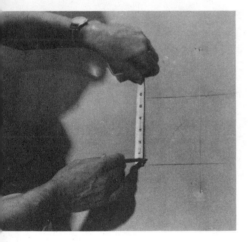

To install a recessed soap dish, locate its position on the wall and cut the opening, avoiding stud locations. Don't locate it in the center of the back wall where your batten strip will be.

Use your level to locate the lowest point of the tub ledge. Your first panel will be here. Next, check the color match and length of all four panels. If there is some variation in length, start with shortest panel. Place ¹⁄₁₆" shims on the tub ledge and place first panel in position on the wall. Small nails are used as shims here. Use a level to plumb the sheet.

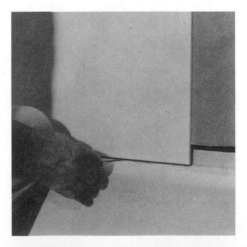

Hold the sheet in position. If the vertical gap between it and the wall is ⅛" or more at any point, use a pencil compass to scribe a vertical line on the sheet edge, using the corner wall as reference. Then do the same along the tub ledge. Trim off the scribed areas with a belt sander.

After trimming, set the fitted panel in position on the shims. Use a pencil to outline the top and side panel edges on the wallboard. Set the panel aside and extend the top edge line around all three walls, using a level. This line will be used to match exactly the height of the other three panels. Draw a line also along the panel edges to indicate where to apply the panel adhesive.

Use an alcohol-dampened cloth to clean the back of the panel, to improve adhesion. Apply neoprene adhesive to the wall with a caulking gun. Place a ¼" bead about an inch from all edges, and apply additional beads vertically about 8" to 10" apart. Within two minutes, press the Corian sheet to the wall.

Pull the panel away from the wall to "string" the adhesive and allow it to vent for about two minutes. Then press it back against the wall and press firmly with the palm of the hand over the entire surface.

Put shims in place and repeat the process for the next panel. If the first panel was on the rear wall, as here, install the other rear panel as shown. If the first panel was an end panel, install the other end panel next. This assures that both panels extend the same distance from the corners. Don't worry about the gap between rear panels, as it will be covered by the batten.

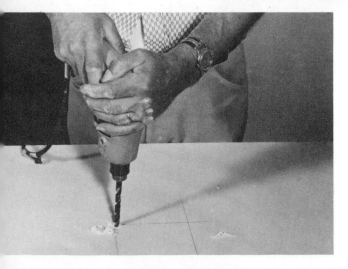

If recessed soap dish is to be installed with this panel, the cutout must be made before it is erected. Locate the exact position in the wallboard and transfer the measurements to the Corian sheet. With electric drill, drill holes in the four corners, inside the lines.

Then use the saber saw to cut from hole to hole, and avoid cutting into the corners with the blade. File to round all corners. Rounded corners are necessary to prevent cracking.

Follow the same procedure as before (see p. 121) to make sure the bottom and corner edges will align, and apply adhesive. Tack a nail into the wallboard to hold the sheet in place until the adhesive sets.

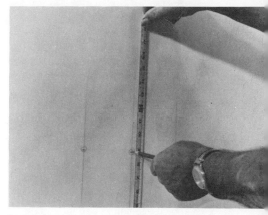

Install the end panel on the wall with no plumbing outlets. Do it as you did the other panels, but leave a $^1/_{16}$" gap at corner for caulk where sheets butt. Install the fourth panel. With shims in place, measure location of the plumbing outlets and transfer them to the front side of the Corian.

Use a hole saw, or drill a hole and use saber saw to cut plumbing holes. Make the holes about ¼" larger than diameter of pipes. Be sure to support the Corian underneath the spots where you drill. File all cut-out edges smooth.

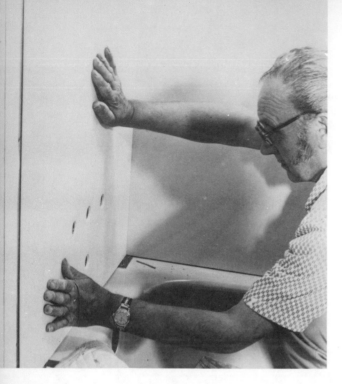

Trial fit, scribe as needed, and install panel.

Installing the batten. Use a level and rule to center batten strip on the rear wall over the gap between panels. Mark the position with strips of masking tape. Don't use pencil, as the lines may show through when final caulking is completed. Trial fit the batten and scribe as needed to match the height of the two rear panels. Trim the scribed area with a belt sander and round the front edges by sanding to eliminate sharp corners. Clean the batten, apply both panel adhesive and sealant as shown, and install batten. Remove the masking tape and promptly remove any excess sealant with alcohol.

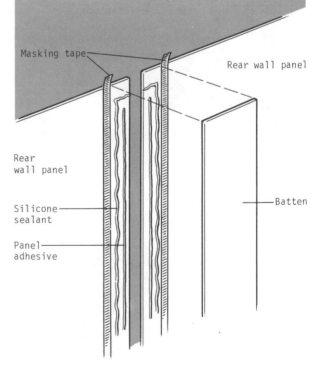

Masking tape

Rear wall panel

Rear wall panel

Batten

Silicone sealant

Panel adhesive

Measure the rear wall above the panels, and cut the 2"x74" trim strip ⅛" shorter than the length of the wall (to leave ¹/₁₆" gaps at each end for caulk). Apply a bead of caulk and adhere it to the wall. Then cut the end panel strips ¹/₁₆" shorter than the required length, and install these strips flush with the front edge of the end wall panels.

Make front edge trim measurements, floor to height of top trim, cut to length and trial fit. Often the trim strips will have to be scribed and trimmed to fit snugly around the tub all the way to the floor.

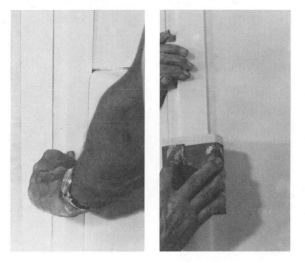

Cut away scribed material on trim with saber saw or belt sander and install.

Clean entire surface before caulking to prevent dust and dirt from getting into sealant. A Scotch-Brite pad will remove pencil marks, surface dirt and scratches and restore original finish. Then check all edges, and go over them with sandpaper to round them. Otherwise, they are sharp enough to cut someone.

Careful caulking of all joints and corners with silicone sealant is necessary for a long-term watertight seal. Remove all shims and nails and fill joints completely. Remove excess sealant with a putty knife. Smooth sealant with a finger or an alcohol-dampened cloth.

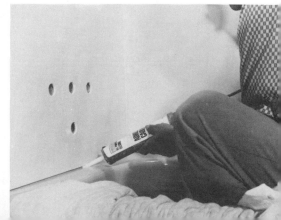

Here's the final job, elegant with faint marbling and easily maintained for many years.

INSTALLING A FIBERGLASS TUB/SHOWER SURROUND. First, while most of them look similar, they are not all fiberglass. The Marlite tub recess kit is made of solid ABS. The Regency Tub Wall is made of solid acrylic. But Universal Rundle, American Standard and others make fiberglass-reinforced tubs and shower receptors which are available in a package with surrounds or without, some of them all one piece and some with up to five pieces.

The all-one-piece models are almost impossible to install in an existing house. But if your new bathroom will be in an addition to your home, they are ideal because you never have to be concerned about seal and caulk lines.

Multi-piece surrounds generally are made with overlapping panels which adjust to spaces that are uneven or out-of-square. In some assemblies, however, these panels are not of equal length. Thus, even if equal panels are required, you still will want to trial fit the panels, scribe a level line on each at the height of the shortest panel, and trim to produce an even line.

Tools you'll need generally include only a trim knife, a drill, a caulking gun, a level and a pencil. And generally, installation procedure is the same for all brands.

The Marlite ABS Tub Recess. This kit includes three 28″x60″ flat panels, two 5″x19″x60″ corner panels, two 6″x18″ filler strips, two 11-ounce cartridges of adhesive and one 4-ounce tube of caulking. It can be applied over any solid surface that is clean and smooth.

The shiplap joinery (overlapping of sheets) makes it suitable for recess areas anywhere from 30″x60″ to 32½″x65½″. But if the back wall is less than 60″ wide or the end walls less than 30″ deep, either can be trimmed down as much as needed. A panel also can be cut down to fit around a window. To install:

1. Center the back panel on the back wall, measuring to get same distance on each side. If the back wall is less than 60″ wide, trim the back panel the same amount. Mark the position of the panel. Check the top edge with a level to make sure it is straight. Trim if it isn't.

2. Apply adhesive to back of panel. Run a continuous ⅛″ bead around perimeter, ½″ from the edge, then in an X or S pattern in center.

3. Position panel on back wall between lines and press against wall. Pull it free of the wall for a minute, then press it back into position, applying palm pressure over the entire surface for a couple of minutes until it sticks.

4. Measure end panels. Front edge of panel should be vertically plumb with face edge of recess. Back edge should be at least 2″ but not more than 4½″ from back wall. Trim if necessary.

5. Measure and mark position of plumbing fittings on flat panel.

6. Draw a circle ¼″ larger than the diameter of each fitting at each point indicated, and cut out with drill or hole saw.

7. Apply adhesive and install, as before. Add bead of adhesive around each hole for plumbing fittings.

Marlite ABS Tub Recess

8. Fit corner panel into position and check fit and lap with flat panels. Remove panel and apply adhesive as before, but include a bead of adhesive around shelf areas.

9. Press corner panel into place, pull away, then press it back into position. Remove excess adhesive with mineral spirits.

10. Seal all edges at tub edge and at top corner of corner panels with caulk. Also caulk inside perimeter of all plumbing fitting openings so a seal will be formed around escutcheon plates when they are replaced. Replace the fittings. The tub leg filler pieces are provided to finish off end wall area extending beyond tub face and below tub ledge.

Wait 15 minutes, then check the entire job for a tight fit and good adhesion. Allow to dry for 24 hours before using.

Completed installation of the Marlite ABS Tub Recess kit.

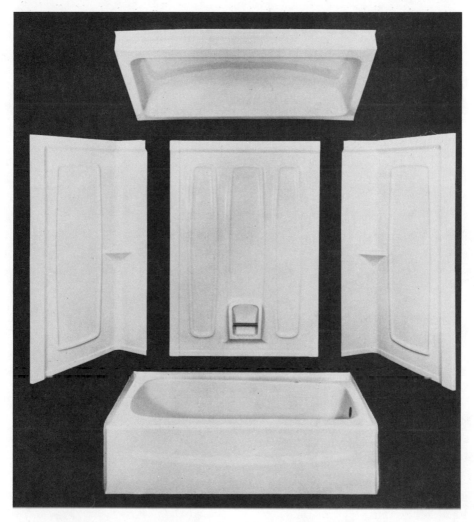

Component parts of Universal Rundle's Combobath. Top is optional.

Universal-Rundle's Combobath. This is a five-piece system that includes either the company's 5′ Neptuna fiberglass tub or its cast-iron tub of the same size. The set also includes an optional top. Installation is basically the same as for other brands except that the end panels go on first and the corners are molded into them. This is a good system for remodeling because the pieces can be brought through the house easily.

Universal-Rundle's Gemini tub and surround system has three pieces including its optional top. It is divided across its width at a point 22″ above the floor and can fit through most doorways.

THE FORMICA 202 SYSTEM. This tub/shower surround system is made not by Formica but by Formco, an unrelated company. It consists of sheets of Formica brand plastic laminate, and becomes a "system" with special moldings and corner pieces to help seal out moisture.

Its great advantages are supreme cleanability, the great variety of patterns and colors, and the suitability of the same material as covering for the other walls of the bathroom. And don't think that will make it look like a kitchen countertop, because all manufacturers of plastic laminates offer dozens of woodgrains and three-dimensional textures.

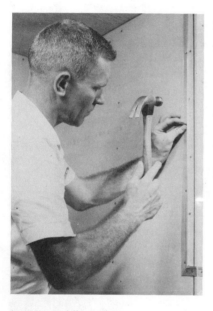

Spread mastic over entire wall with roller.

Install moldings in corners and at edges around windows. Cut to fit with a hacksaw.

Slip edge of laminate sheet into molding and press against wall. Note cutouts have already been made for soap dishes.

Roll every inch to insure good adhesive contact.

Finish off with decorative strip over front exposed edges.

A completed Formco installation.

For those who like a wood look on the bathroom walls, Masonite Corp.'s "Mini-Planks." They are ¼" thick, of hardboard finished with melamine and only 16" wide. They can be installed over just about any surface. Panels come with adhesive and metal clips and have tongue-and-groove joinery. This makes them self-aligning and conceals all clips. You simply cut planks to desired height, spread the adhesive, slip the clips into place and nail to the wall.

Another wall paneling made for high-humidity areas is Masonite's Royaltile. It has a plastic finish on core of ⅛" tempered hardboard, and is used in tub area as well as on other walls. Panels are mounted with mastic, and prefinished corner moldings interlock to provide waterproof installation.

Marlite's brick panels actually are made of fiberglass, but it's hard to tell it. Panels come in 12–brick units and are self-aligning. A panel weighs two pounds.

10 | Floors

THE IMPORTANT THINGS to remember about the bathroom floor are that the material must be moisture-resistant, and a sound floor is needed under the surfacing. The room is a high-traffic area so you want a floor covering that will wear well.

In many modern houses the basic floor consists of no more than $1/2''$ plywood laid on the floor joists. This is not enough to support ceramic tile without later cracking of the grout lines, so for tile you would have to add a sheet of at least $3/8''$ plywood, hardboard or, best, $1/2''$ Wonder-Board, a concrete glass-fiber-reinforced underlayment made for this purpose by American Olean.

The modern trend toward use of carpet might seem inconsistent with the need for moisture resistance, but carpeting used in the bathroom is made of synthetic materials that do resist moisture. Nevertheless, many brands will allow some moisture to penetrate, so the floor must be sound and sealed. If wall-to-wall carpet will be used, an excellent material is kitchen carpeting, which has an impermeable membrane between the nap and the rubber cushion. Note that this is not the same as indoor-outdoor carpet, although many carpet salesmen think it is. Indoor-outdoor carpet allows for easy penetration of water rather than resisting it.

The new cushioned resilient sheet vinyls are ideal for the bathroom floor. They are easy to clean, never need waxing, permit no moisture penetration, and they are soft and warm underfoot. And dropped bottles are less likely to break. Professional installation is recommended for many of them, but that won't daunt the handy do-it-yourselfer who is reasonably careful in his work.

Vinyl asbestos tile and vinyl tile are popular and easy to lay. Cork, rubber and asphalt tiles are also available, but they are not as durable.

LAYING A CERAMIC TILE FLOOR. First, buy enough tile to do the job, allowing for some breakage and a few mistakes in cutting. You don't want to be forced to stop near the end of the job and run out for more tile. See Chapter 9 for general information about tile.

Be prepared to consult with the tile dealer regarding the condition and nature of the floor. It's a good idea to take a sketch with you, so the dealer can help lay it out and make recommendations. You will need certain round-edge tiles as well as the main spacer tiles, and you might want some coved pieces at the walls.

And remember, these are general instructions, intended to let you know what is involved in the job. Be sure to read and follow the manufacturer's instructions in doing the job.

Tile-setting tools include a straightedge, tape rule, chalk line, square, sandpaper, cleaning rags, a tile cutter, notched trowel, rubber trowel or squeegee, and tile nipper. These usually can be rented from the tile dealer.

You can tile over any structurally sound, dry, clean and level surface. But don't try it over a springy floor. If you have any doubts at all, add a sheet of 3/8" exterior-grade plywood, use a primer, and seal edges before nailing in place. Use 6d ring-shank nails every 6" along floor joists, and allow 1/8" expansion joints between the plywood edges and walls. Fill the expansion joints with tile adhesive.

It is possible to nip the tile to fit around the toilet, but it is far better to remove the toilet, then simply to omit one tile at the toilet flange that leads into the soil pipe.

If you use Wonder-Board for the underlayment, sizes available, all 1/2" thick, are 30"x60", 36"x48", 36"x60" and 36"x72". You need no special tools. You cut it by scoring and snapping, and at the toilet flange you simply knock a hole in it with a hammer.

To lay the Wonder-Board, apply a bead of high-strength, waterproof construction adhesive on the back side, around the entire perimeter about 1/2" from the edge and in an X from corner to corner, and through the center from end to end and side to side. It is a good idea then to apply spots of adhesive in all segments.

Put the panel in place and nail it down every 12" to 16" around the perimeter and along the joists, to hold it in place while the adhesive sets.

To tile the floor, start somewhere in the middle. Snap chalk lines from wall to wall to wall in both directions, making sure with your square that they cross at right angles, and then loose lay a row of tile in both directions to make sure you don't end up with less than half a tile at any wall. Readjust your chalk lines if necessary.

Apply the adhesive with a notched trowel, being careful not to cover up your directional lines, starting from where the lines cross. Hold the trowel at a 45° angle for 100% coverage, and spread only a little at a time so the adhesive doesn't dry until the tile is set.

Set each tile with a slight twisting motion and press firmly into place. Most tile has built-in spacers to assure a straight grout line between, but if your tile doesn't have them be sure you keep the lines straight.

Clean off excess adhesive on the face of the tile right away.

Chances are the corners of the room aren't perfectly square, so don't cut a whole row of end pieces at one time. Cut them one by one as you come to them. You'll use the tile nipper to shape tiles around any pipes. Nip off little bits at a time.

On Wonder-Board, use a floor-type, presanded dry-set or latex portland cement mortar to set the tile. First, trowel on a skim-coat of mortar, forcing it into all the little openings of the concrete surface, using the back of the trowel rather than the notched edge. Then lay a coat with the notched edge.

Trowel notches should be 1/4"x1/4"x1/4" for regular floor tile. For tiles with larger ribs or uneven backs, quarry tile or slate, it should be 3/8"x1/4"x1/4".

After 24 hours you can begin grouting. Work the grout into the joints with the rubber trowel or squeegee, and strike the grout lines with the handle of a toothbrush.

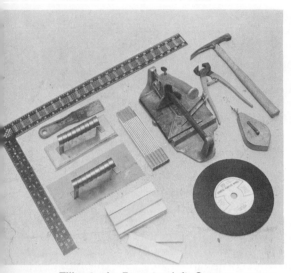

Tiling tools. From top left: Square, scraper (for removing adhesive stains on non-waxed tiles), rubber trowel (for spreading grout), notched trowel (for spreading adhesive), plywood spacers (for tile without spacerlugs), ruler, tile cutter, sandpaper, tile nipper, chalk line, and hammer.

Materials: 6″x6″ quarry tiles, ceramic floor tile adhesive (both from American Olean), and brown Acid-R portland cement grout by L&M. A coat of sealer (not shown) can be applied to unglazed tiles before beginning work to simplify grout clean-up.

To make a final decision on tiling pattern, tiles are laid out on location.

Here, installation begins along the longest and most visible wall because room is slightly out-of-square. This way, tile fragments will be needed only along the opposite, less visible side of room.

Adhesive is spread with notched trowel over a small area at a time. Tiles are placed with a slight twisting motion so that adhesive gets into grooves of tile.

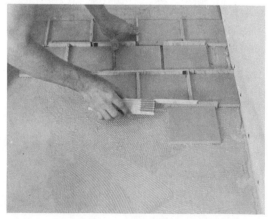

Masonry blade on radial-arm saw is a good way to score this type of tile. Tile is scored to approximately ⅓ its depth. Mask and goggles are necessary safety precautions since dust will be very fine.

Notch is finished off with Remington Grit–Edge hacksaw blade.

Grout width around obstructions should match grouting between other tiles.

A sharp rap with hammer will knock out scored area. Jagged edges should be smoothed with sandpaper.

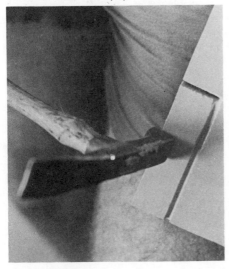

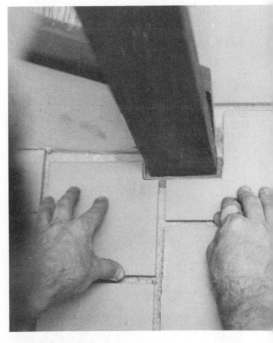

Another obstruction. Here, it was easier to trim tiles to fit around sides of toilet base than to remove it. Trimmed tiles are large enough that there is no noticeable disruption in the pattern.

Grout is applied to small area at a time with rubber trowel.

Tile surface is then wiped clean of grout with clean wet rags. Muriatic acid will remove grout stains from tile.

Finally, tile sealer is applied.

For ceramic mosaics, glazed or unglazed, 2" square or less, use a sand-latex-portland cement grout. Or you can use one part sand, one part portland cement, properly damp-cured. To damp-cure, cover it for at least three days with a plastic film after wetting it down the first day after grouting. (It's easier to use the latex mixture.)

For other glazed floor tile, use a good quality dry-set wall grout with a latex additive.

For quarry tile or slate, or any other with a joint 1/8" or wider, use sand and portland properly damp-cured, or a ready-mix such as Upco's Hydroment, L&M's Acid-R, or Tec Joint Filler.

INSTALLING A CUSHIONED RESILIENT SHEET FLOOR. As noted, there are some cushioned sheet vinyls for which the manufacturer recommends professional installation. But that doesn't mean you can't do it.

Here is Armstrong's "Interflex" system for installing two such floor coverings, Premier Sundial and Tredway. Both come in rolls, but Tredway can be folded like a blanket (for up to three hours only) for easier transport home in the family car. Both are cushioned, no-wax vinyls.

If you carry Tredway home folded, you must then unfold it and roll it tightly, face out, and store it that way overnight before installing. Temperature should be 65° or higher.

To install on wood or particleboard, you will use a staple gun and heavy duty 3/8" to 1/2" staples. For areas where you can't staple, such as in the kick space of a vanity cabinet, you will use adhesive. On concrete, you use adhesive only.

Over wood, the only tools you will need are a straight-blade utility knife, metal straightedge or carpenter's square, staple gun and staples, hammer and screwdriver or putty knife. If you will have any seams, buy the appropriate seam-sealing kit, S-820 for Premier Sundial or S-555 for Tredway. If you will need adhesive, buy Armstrong's S-660 Trowelable Interflex Adhesive.

1. Clear the room of movable objects, and repair any major damage in the floor. When you use adhesive, be sure there is no flame and that you have ventilation.

2. Remove any quarter-round molding, and make sure floor is clean. Even a fine layer of dust will render the finest adhesive useless.

3. The material comes in 6' and 12' rolls, so it is unlikely you will need two pieces in a bathroom. Lay the material out roughly in place in the bathroom. If it is too big to handle easily, trim it, but there should be at least 3" excess material at each wall.

4. The first obvious problem will be the toilet. Make sure the material is in place around the remainder of the bathroom, with a little excess folded up along the walls, then locate the edge directly behind the toilet. Make a neat cut from the edge to the point directly in front of the toilet and precisely where it meets the floor, then push the material down around the toilet.

5. The fit around the toilet will probably be highly visible and is the most critical part of your installation. Using the carpenter square, press down on the material directly against the toilet and make a small cut with the straightedge utility knife. Move the square, repeat and make another small cut. You will be dealing with rounded corners of the toilet, so keep the cuts small to keep the rounded appearance. Go completely around the toilet in this way.

6. With that done, proceed to the corners of the room nearest the toilet. Smooth the material, press down into the corner, push the knife into the corner and cut straight up through the excess material. Then you can use your square to push the material down and cut along the wall.

7. Proceed around the room. If there is an outside corner, fold the material back so it meets the corner diagonally, push the knife into the corner and cut upward through the excess. Then cut along the walls.

8. Now that the floor covering has been trimmed to fit accurately all around, it must be fastened down to the floor within two hours. This is because the material has a temporary pliancy built in that enables you to

Installation of Premier Sundial cushioned sheet vinyl (Manchester Brick pattern). Material is laid out roughly in place, with a margin of 3" at each wall.

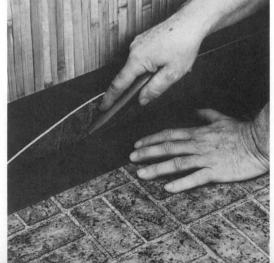

Metal straightedge is used to push edges of sheet snugly against edge of wall. Material is then trimmed with utility knife.

stretch it where you may have cut imperfectly. A delay longer than two hours wastes this feature. Staple it all around, with staples 3″ apart, close enough to the wall for quarter round molding to hide the staples. But if there are any places that need adhesive, such as the cut behind the toilet or in the vanity kickspace, apply the adhesive before stapling. Where adhesive is used, fold the material back and trowel on a three-inch band, then press it into place and roll it with a hand roller.

9. If you are installing on concrete or some other hard surface that you can't staple, use adhesive all around. Start by folding back a corner, then start spreading the three-inch band of adhesive one foot from the corner, going away from the corner. Proceed to one foot from the next corner, fold it back and start again one foot from the corner. Go back and do the corners last, until you have the band of adhesive around the entire perimeter. Again, roll the edge down into the adhesive.

10. Replace quarter rounds or wall base moldings and install metal threshold strips in doorways.

11. If the surface appears to have uneven or loose-fitting areas right after installing, allow it to contract overnight before placing anything heavy on it. It is built to contract and take up any such looseness.

Remember, this material is anchored only around the perimeter, so don't try to slide heavy objects over it. Use a sheet of hardboard for any such sliding.

The completed Premier Sundial installation. Staples around perimeter are concealed by molding.

An advantage of resilient sheet flooring is that it can look like imported clay tile, as this pattern by Armstrong does, or simulate wood or other materials.

INSTALLING CARPET. Kitchen carpet is a good floor covering for the bathroom because it has an impermeable membrane between the nap and cushion that prevents penetration of moisture.

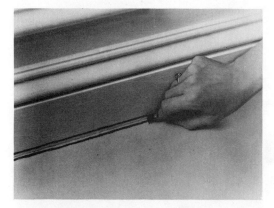

To trim carpet, make a heavy crayon or chalk mark along the floor and wall.

Press carpet into the corner so it picks up the lines, then cut.

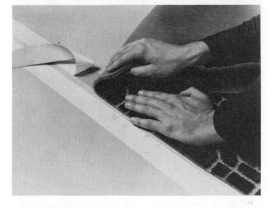

Use two-sided tape to hold it down along perimeter and seams.

You can also use carpet squares on the bathroom floor. These are Armstrong 12″x12″ self-sticking squares. With a tweedy pattern such as this, there is no problem in matching squares.

11 | Ceilings

PLAIN OLD PAINT has always been the almost universal option for ceiling treatments. But there are also two other treatments — plastic laminate and ceiling tile — and there is good reason for them. They can give the room's decor a more unified look, and, of course, they cover flaws much more effectively than paint. Plastic laminate can be matched to the countertop or vanity cabinet. Ceiling tiles are available in a number of styles to complement any decor. They can be glued directly to the ceiling to cover up minor flaws, such as the cracks caused by settling of the building, or to make the room quieter. They can also be installed on furring strips or on a suspension system to cover major flaws or to save heat.

PLASTIC LAMINATE. This is one of the miracle materials of our age, and it is not too difficult for the do-it-yourselfer to install. It looks best in a one-piece installation, and that means 5'x12' or less. You'll have to cut it in another room and move it into the bathroom, which is a problem in itself. The piece will have to be trimmed at least 1/2" in each dimension to make sure you have space to move it up into place. You can use ordinary mastic, or contact adhesive. Either will work, but most professionals use contact adhesive. It will be a lot of work to get the sheet into the room and up into position. On the other hand, you will gain a ceiling that is totally impervious to moisture damage, and there are more than a hundred patterns and colors to choose from. It is well worth considering.

But ceiling tiles are easier. Let's consider them. There are four ways to install a tile ceiling, or five if you count a variation. All are relatively easy for the do-it-yourselfer. Installation procedures for each method are described in the following pages to give an idea of the work involved. Complete details are also supplied by tile manufacturers.

CEMENTING TILE DIRECTLY TO THE CEILING. The only tools you'll need are a stepladder, chalk line, tape measure, hammer, brush, staple gun and razor-blade knife. You'll also need a saw and miter box to cut the decorative molding used to finish the job off.

You'll have to buy the ceiling tile, brush-on ceiling cement, molding and finishing nails.

Armstrong packs complete instructions in every package of ceiling tile. The tiles are 12"x12", or 1'x4'. To find out how much tile you need simply measure the ceiling in both directions and multiply one dimension by the other. This gives you the number of square feet, which will be the number of 12"x12" tiles you will need. Divide by four to get the

Cementing Tile Directly to the Ceiling

number of 1'x4' tiles. If there are any offsets in the ceiling, measure them separately in the same way and add the totals.

The ceiling must be sound and level.

1. Remove any flaking paint or loose wallpaper.

2. Calculate the size of border tiles along each wall, so that they will be even along opposite walls. The border tiles on each wall will cover half the number of inches left over in each direction. That is, if one dimension of the ceiling is 14'8", one row of tiles will take 14 full tiles and a 4" tile at each end for the border.

3. Snap a chalk line to align the first row of border tiles along two adjacent walls from the corner in which you will start tiling. Be sure they intersect at a right angle.

4. Cut the first four or five border tiles to size for both walls in your starting corner. Don't cut all border tiles at once, because there may be wall variations for which you will have to adjust. Cut then as you go along.

5. Place five daubs of cement on the first border tile, a daub in each corner and one in the center.

6. Fit it into position in your starting corner, making sure the stapling flange is lined up on the chalk line.

7. Insert a couple of staples into each flange. This is to hold the tile in position while the adhesive dries.

8. Work across the ceiling, installing two or three border tiles at a time and then filling in between them with full-size tiles.

9. When you reach the opposite wall, individually measure and cut each tile to fit.

10. Finally, nail up the wall molding to finish it off.

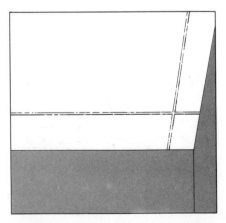

Measure room to determine size of border tiles. Border tiles should match those on opposite side of the room.

Draw in chalk lines for border tiles, making sure that lines intersect at a right angle.

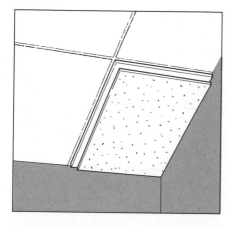

Apply cement and place first border tile in position, lining up staple flange on chalk lines.

Insert two staples into each flange to hold tiles in position while the cement dries.

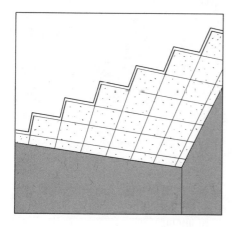

Continue across ceiling, installing two or three border tiles at a time, then filling in with full-size tiles.

Finally, nail up the wall molding.

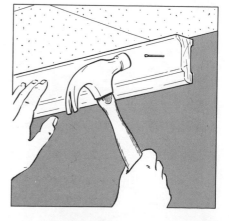

The Furring Strip Method

Unsound or unlevel ceilings. If plaster on the ceiling is cracked in some areas, or if the ceiling isn't level or if there is no ceiling—just exposed joists—you still can cement ceiling tile directly to the ceiling by first putting up furring strips.

Furring strips are available at most home centers, and come in lengths of 8', 10' and 12'.

Procedure is basically the same as for the first method, except that you will nail up the furring strips across the entire ceiling, perpendicular to the joists and into the joists, to provide a solid base for the ceiling tiles and to correct irregularities or level the ceiling.

First you will have to calculate the size of the border tiles along the two walls that are perpendicular to the joists. Nail up the first furring strip so that the stapling flange of the first row of border tiles will be in the center of the furring strip. The remainder of the furring strips will be 12" apart, from center to center, with an additional strip for the border tile on the opposite wall.

With furring strips, you will not use adhesive. Proceed as before, stapling the tiles through the flanges into the furring strips. The tiles are tongue-and-grooved to fit together and give you a nice, even ceiling.

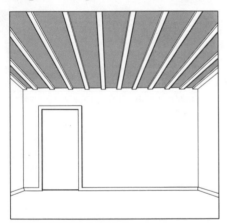

Furring strips are nailed to joists.

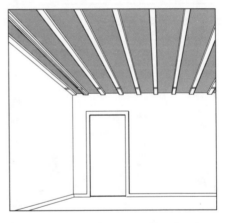

Chalk lines are drawn to align border tiles In each direction.

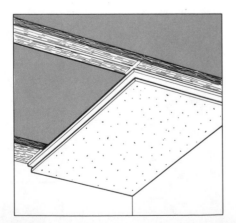

First border tile is lined up where the chalk lines intersect, and its flange stapled to the furring strip.

THE INTEGRID SYSTEM. There's nothing wrong with wood furring strips. But it does take a lot of time and measuring to put them up, and many do-it-yourselfers have trouble with all of the overhead nailing required.

Armstrong's Integrid system eliminates 95% of the overhead nailing. It is a lightweight, interlocking metal framework that provides a hidden support system for the company's Chandelier or Trendsetter ceiling tiles. The framework consists of furring channel, wall molding, and cross tee pieces, with springs to butt the tiles tightly together. The only additional tool you will need is a hacksaw, or metal snips.

These tiles have tongue-and-flange edges that fit together, as do many other ceiling tiles, but there also is a kerf, or slot, into which the cross tee fits. You won't have to worry about matching border tiles because when these tiles are fitted together the joints do not show.

1. Snap a chalk line across the wall, perpendicular to the joist direction, 26" from the wall, and nail up the first furring channel into the joists. Furring channel takes a nail every 48".

2. Nail up the other channels 4' apart.

3. Nail up the metal wall molding ¾" below the furring channels, or 2" below the ceiling, all around.

4. Lay the first four 12"x12" tiles or the first 1'x4' tile in place at starting corner, on the wall molding. Clip a 48" cross tee into the furring channel, sliding it into the concealed kerfs of the tiles.

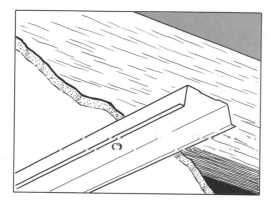

The first furring channel is positioned 26" from the wall and nailed into the joists.

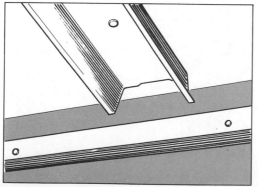

Wall molding is nailed ¾" below the channel all the way around the room.

The Integrid System

5. At the end of each row, cut tile slightly short to make room for wall spring that you insert between tile and wall to keep tiles butted tight together. When you cut end tile to fit, use the remainder to start next row of tile, and continue across room.

6. Cut the last tile slightly short on two sides so you can jockey it up through the hole and into place.

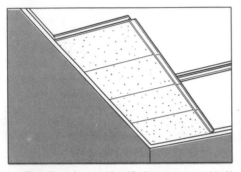

The first four 12″x12″ tiles (or one 1′x4′ tile) are placed on wall molding.

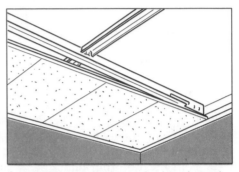

Cross tee is snapped onto furring channel.

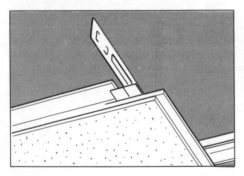

Cross tee then slides into kerfs of tiles to lock tiles in place.

Installation continues across the room in the same way—each four tiles (or one 1′x4′ tile) secured by the wall molding and cross tee pieces; wall spring inserted at the end of each row.

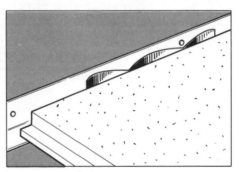

At the end of each row, a wall spring is placed between tile and wall.

The last tile is trimmed on two sides and jockeyed into place.

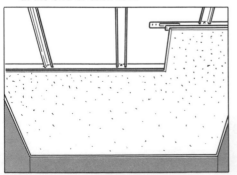

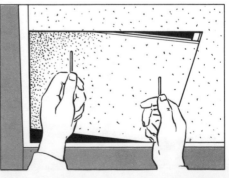

SUSPENDING THE CEILING. A suspended ceiling is somewhat more complicated. For it you use a light metal grid system suspended from the old ceiling with wires. Actually, you can suspend the Integrid system with wires to lower the ceiling, if you wish. The advantage would be the same continuous look of the regular Integrid system.

In other suspended ceilings the framework shows, and the ceiling tiles are 2'x2' or 2'x4'. Lighting units are made to match either size, and you can buy them with the tiles. You must allow at least 6″ between the old and new ceiling for a lighting unit, and wire the fixtures first.

You can make an entire suspended ceiling luminous, a fine touch for a bathroom and no more difficult than a regular suspended ceiling with opaque tiles.

Materials. You will need main tees and cross tees, and wall moldings, or angles. The main tees and wall angles come in 12' lengths. Cross tees come in 4' and 2' lengths. If you have to put two pieces of main tee together, as you would for a ceiling more than 12' long, you will need splicers. You will need enough wall angle for the entire perimeter of the room. You will need enough main tees to place one every 4' across the joists. The cross tees will be placed at 2' intervals. Then you will need the proper number of ceiling tiles, in either 2'x2' or 2'x4' sizes. If you use 2'x2' tiles, you will also need enough 2' cross tees to divide each 4' space in half. So make a sketch of your ceiling on graph paper and calculate the materials needed. You will need enough suspension wire to hang a length every 3 or 4 feet in each direction—each length 12″ longer than the distance from old to new ceiling.

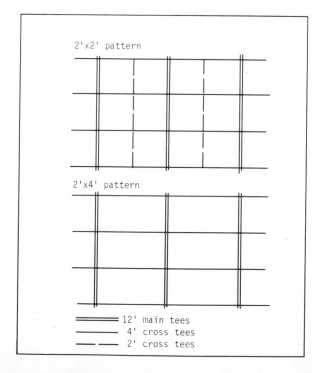

2'x2' pattern

2'x4' pattern

═══════ 12' main tees
─────── 4' cross tees
─ ─ ─ ─ 2' cross tees

A preliminary sketch on graph paper is useful in deciding which size of tile to use, and will also indicate quantity of materials needed. If 2'x4' tiles are used, grid pattern can be either standard (4' side parallel to short dimension of room), or reversed (4″ side perpendicular to short dimension). In either case, main tees are spaced every 4' across the joists.

Suspending the Ceiling

1. Snap a chalk line around the room at the height of the new ceiling, checking lines with a level. Nail up the wall angle so the bottom flange is at the level line. Nail firmly to studs.

2. At inside corners, overlap wall angle. At outside corners, if any, make a miter cut.

3. Main tees will be 4' apart, at right angles to the joists, and they will hang from the suspension wires. First locate the points where you will hang the main tees and stretch a tight string from wall angle to wall angle at each main tee point. These will be your guides for the length of the suspension wires as well.

4. Locate point of first suspension wire for each main tee—directly above the point where the first cross tee will cross it. In the ceiling above place a screw eye or hook, or a nail from which to hang the wire. Attach other hooks every 4' along the level line.

5. Cut the suspension wires, making each one 12″ longer than the distance from the hook to the main tee.

6. Secure each wire to the hook above, pull to remove any kinks, and make a 90° bend in each one at the point where it meets the guide strings you have stretched across.

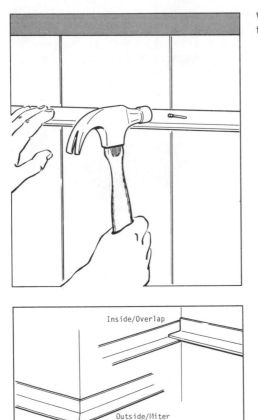

Wall angle is attached so that bottom flange meets level line.

Inside/Overlap

Outside/Miter

Wall angle pieces are mitered at outside corners and overlapped at inside corners.

7. Most main tees have slots for cross tees punched every 12″, beginning 6″ from each end. Check your sketch for the distance from the wall to the first cross tee, and measure this distance along the top flange of the main tee. Locate the slot just beyond that point, then measure back from the slot the same distance, subtracting ⅛″ to allow for the thickness of the wall angle. Saw main tee at this point. When main tees are installed in rooms less than 12′ across, they are trimmed to the exact measurement of the room less ¼″ for the two wall angles.

8. If room is larger than 12′, use splice, but be sure to align the splice so the suspension wires still are positioned correctly, or main tees will be thrown off.

9. Install main tees on suspension wires at height of 90° bend you have made, but check them also with a level after twisting wire excess up along wire. Use pliers to make the loop tight at the main tee; otherwise the loops will make it difficult to seat the panels later.

10. Insert cross tees in the slots in the main tees. If cross tee has a lock

Strings attached to tops of wall angles stretch across room to mark main tee positions.

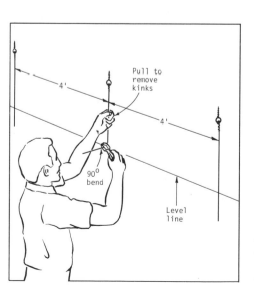

Suspension wires are attached to ceiling every 4′ along level line. Wire is bent with pliers at 90° angle at level of guide strings.

Suspending the Ceiling

tab, be sure it is outside the slot. Position cross tees for the length of panels.

11. Install border cross tees between the wall angle and the last main tee.

12. Place panels by tilting them to lift them above grid, then lowering them into position.

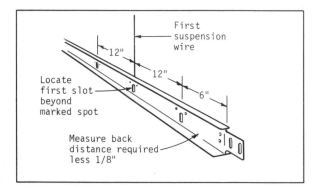

Point where cross tees will attach to main tee slots is determined. If room dimension is less than 12', main tees are carefully measured and trimmed so that connecting parts will line up.

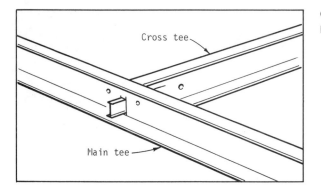

Cross tees are inserted in slots provided in main tee.

These 2'x4' panels look like wood, but they are made of mineral fiber which holds its shape in bathroom extremes of temperature and humidity. They are washable. Armstrong.

Sculptured plaster is the impression given by these acoustical ceiling tiles, adding to the Victorian decor. They are "Victoria," by Armstrong.

12 | Lighting, Ventilation, and Heating

THE THOUGHT AND THE funding for the bathrooms of most homes usually go into plumbing fixtures. Far too little goes into lighting design or other mechanical functions such as venting and heat.

Lighting, however, is an important element of design, and planning for lighting should always take into account the placement of plumbing fixtures, the color scheme and the type of mirror. Placement of fixtures is pertinent to placement of lighting equipment because light colors in small bathrooms reflect useful light into the user's face, whereas a dark surface absorbs light. Also, a medicine cabinet mirror necessitates different lighting solutions than larger mirrors.

Lighting in the bathroom should fulfill specific needs:

1. There should be plenty of light at the mirror for shaving, grooming hair, applying make-up, etc.

2. There should be general light for overall vision and to supplement local lighting.

3. A reading and rest light over toilet and tub is needed for those who use the room as a library.

4. A vapor-proof fixture over the tub or shower is needed for vision and safety.

5. Consideration also should be given to special-purpose lights, such as heat or sun lamps or a pedicure light under the vanity counter.

LIGHTING FIXTURES. Overhead light is needed for hair care. Lights on both sides of the mirror are needed for face care.

Small medicine cabinets, 12″ to 24″ wide, often have their own lights on both sides, or permit use of wall brackets spaced 30″ apart and 60″ above the floor. These should be used in conjunction with an overhead light centered over the front edge of the lavatory.

The trend toward mirroring the entire wall or toward large mirrors over 3′ wide makes a small bathroom seem larger, but it pushes side fixtures too far apart to be effective. So such wide mirrors call for wider overhead lighting such as soffit or cornice fixtures.

A soffit may be either an existing hollow, boxed-in space over the counter where the ceiling has been furred down, or you may build a shallow box. Both are simple do-it-yourself projects. The soffit should be 8″ to 12″ high and 16″ to 20″ deep, and at least 48″ wide. Fluorescent tubes are excellent for this.

Another type of structural lighting easy to build is the open-topped soffit, or canopy. The canopy light needs the same dimensions as the soffit, but is installed 12″ down from the ceiling. This not only lights the user's face effectively, but also provides general room illumination.

A theatrical technique is to use incandescent strip fixtures on either side of the mirror, 30″ apart, and another strip along the top of the mirror. For this use bare, low-wattage globes, four 25-watt bulbs per strip or six 15-watt bulbs per strip.

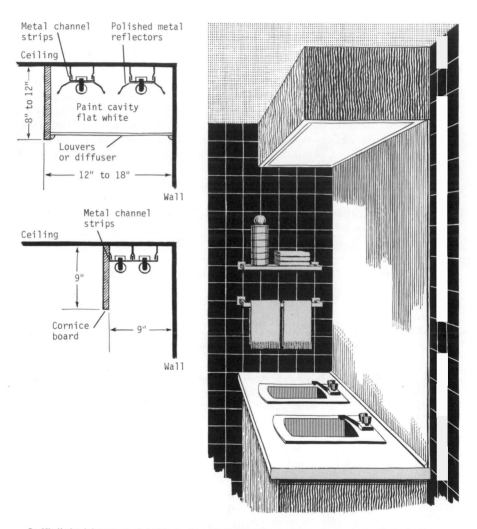

Soffit light (shown at right) is built with light-diffuser type glass or plastic in bottom to provide good light for grooming. It is easy to build yourself with two 40W fluorescent tubes that rest on metal channel strips attached to ceiling (see cross-sectional view at top).

Cornice light is also a good system over a wide mirror. Here, fluorescent tubes are moved away from wall close to cornice.

When soffit, canopy or cornice lighting is used, it often is advisable to add lights in decorative sconces on either side of the mirror. These are mostly for esthetic value, but if installed with a dimmer switch they also are good for a night-light.

Soffit light in furred down ceiling gives a wash of light with its two rows of fluorescent tubes. Niche in background has its own overhead grooming light in hollow ceiling cavity.

Supplementary light source is used here for benefit of the potted plants. Low wattage Westinghouse Agro-Lite reflector bulbs are housed in clamp-on or portable fixtures.

Any light over the tub should be a recessed, vapor-proof housing with a 75-watt or 100-watt bulb. The switch should be remote, for safety reasons.

For the luxury of a pedicure light, consider a small bullet housing, directional, with a 50-watt reflector bulb under the front edge of the vanity cabinet.

The "Light for Living" guidelines of the American Home Lighting Institute recommend 100 to 150 watts of incandescent light or 60 to 80 watts fluorescent for general illumination in the bathroom, in addition to mirror lighting. For a reader, a 75-watt down light is recommended.

For mirror lighting, the Guidelines recommend multiple incandescent bulbs totaling 120 to 180 watts, or a 20-watt fluorescent fixture on each side of the mirror.

Incandescent lighting. Incandescent bulbs give a warm light with quite a bit of red in it, flattering to complexions. Higher wattage bulbs are more efficient than lower, but long-life bulbs usually sacrifice some light output in favor of the extra hours of life, so use them where bulb replacement is difficult. In reflector and PAR bulbs which direct light to where it is wanted, lower wattages are more efficient.

Recessed fluorescent fixture provides generous mirror and room lighting, and an additional vapor-proof fixture in tub area gives adequate light for bathing when curtains are drawn.

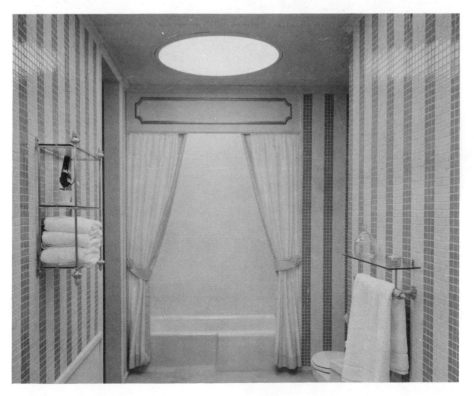

This bathroom in a Westinghouse energy-saver house uses a prismatic wrap-around fixture with one fluorescent 40W tube.

Built-in canopy lighting with Vita-Lite tubes by Dura-Lite, which simulate sunlight. Similar tubes are installed behind translucent panel at left to keep plants healthy and also to provide general illumination.

Two 20W Vita-Lite tubes are used in this overhead canopy, to illuminate vanity area as well as plants. Incandescent fixture at left is decorative and provides general room light.

This "jungle" in an all-tile bath is kept healthy by bathroom heat, humidity, and Vita-Lites in soffit over grooming area.

Fluorescent lighting. Fluorescent tubes produce two to four times as much light per watt as incandescent bulbs, and they last much longer. Their life is determined not by the number of hours they burn, but by the number of times they are started. As an example, one Westinghouse Ultralume tube rated at 10,000 hours average life, based on three hours per start, will last for 18,000 hours if it burns 12 hours per start, or 22,000 hours if it burns continuously. On the other hand, while you would save on tubes by burning continously, you might not be able to pay your electric bill.

Fluorescents generally give a cooler light than incandescents, and most suitable for the home are Deluxe Warm White, Deluxe Cool White and Natural. If your bathroom needs a warm light for reds, yellows and browns, the Vita-Lite by Duro-Lite, designed as a plant light, is excellent for pleasing color rendition.

While fluorescents put out more light per watt, the saving is not as much as it appears to be, because the ballast also uses some electricity. But even so, you get more for your money with fluorescents.

Efficiency of a light source is measured by the amount of lumens per watt it produces. Here's a comparison:

Light Source	Lumens Per Watt	Average Rated Life
Incandescent, 15-250 W	10-20	750-2500 hours
Fluorescent, 15-40 W	30-80	7500-18,000 hours
Mercury, Deluxe White, 40-250 W°	40-60	10,000-24,000 hours

° This requires warm-up time, hence is not suited to indoor use

VENTILATION. Bathrooms need mechanical ventilation. A window alone cannot effect adequate air exchange.

Ventilation removes moisture, excess heat, health-related gaseous and aerosol pollutants, and odors. It also contributes to better insulation, since moisture buildup within walls reduces effectiveness of insulation.

You measure the effectiveness of a bathroom ventilator by the cubic feet per minute (CFM) it moves. This should be exhausted to the outside. The Home Ventilating Institute, which sets standards for home ventilation, recommends a fan capable of eight air changes per hour for the bathroom. Or, more specifically, with a standard 8' ceiling, multiply the square feet in the bathroom by 1.07 to find the CFM capacity you need. Here are some typical figures:

Square Feet in Bathroom	CFM Mimimum
40	35
50	45
60	55
70	65
80	75
90	85
100	95
110	105

Any bathroom ventilator you buy should have a CFM rating on it, and it is a good idea to choose a more powerful one than the mimimum recommendation.

This is the "Millionair" by Broan; heat, light and ventilation in one unit. It has two motors; one for heat and one for venting.

But another important point is that no fan can move air out of the bathroom unless the room gets make-up air. That is, there must be as much air flowing into the room as the fan is trying to move out. Opening a window a little, or a door, normally doesn't accomplish this because the fan will draw air directly from that opening without exhausting room air. So the easy solution is to cut an inch off the bottom of the bathroom door, then place the fan in the ceiling or on the wall opposite, as far as possible from the opening.

This Broan unit combines venting and light, but not heat.

A unit that disguises its functions is this heat-light-vent unit by NuTone. Its switch plate has three separate switches, and it is rated at 70 CFM.

Yes, you can get heat by itself— no light, no vent. This, by Broan, mounts in wall, draws 1430 watts and gives 4500 btu per hour, and is easy to install.

Ceiling fans can discharge upward, vertically, using 6″ or 7″ round duct. But if your bathroom is on an outside wall you can buy one with a side discharge, which usually uses 4″ round duct.

There are other side-discharge fans designed to be installed in a wall between studs or in a ceiling between joists. These take a 3″ round duct. Wall fans designed to vent directly through the wall without a duct run should have a weatherproof hood to protect against rain, snow and outside air.

Here is how a representative ceiling fan unit (the NuTone Heat-A-Ventlite) is vented. Duct can go directly to outside wall, or elbow up through roof. 90° turn diminishes air movement.

Roof cap

6″ duct

Wall cap

4″ duct

In all cases, follow manufacturer recommendations on duct size, and always duct to the outside by the shortest, most direct route. Each foot of duct diminishes the effectiveness of the fan, and so does each turn.

HEATING. Most older homes have heat in existing bathrooms. Many newer homes don't. In a new bathroom you may find it easy to extend the home heat system to the bathroom. Before you do, though, remember that you would be heating a room that is used only intermittently. There may be a better way.

One of the ideal appliances for the home in recent years has been the combination light-heat-vent unit that fits into the ceiling. It can put heat into the bathroom when you need it, but only when you need it, so it is an energy saver.

Some of these units provide electric resistance heat blown into the bathroom by a fan. Others use heat bulbs. There is a further energy-saving advantage to infra-red heat bulbs that heat by radiation, because these do not heat the entire room. Rather, they heat a selected area when you enter the room and turn them on. Typically, one of these will run 250 watts and need a porcelain socket if installed separately, but they also are available in the combination heat-light-vent units. The combination units usually have a timer switch.

13 | Safety in the Bathroom

EACH YEAR, more than 50,000 persons in this country are injured in bathtub falls, and many others are hurt in minor ways simply because there isn't enough light to see adequately. Others die due to electrical shock in wet bathroom conditions.

First, consider the tub. Most new tubs have slip-resistant bottoms. Fiberglass tubs are naturally more slip resistant. But when the bottom is soapy in either case, slips result.

Older tubs can be made more slip-free by addition of decorative anti-skid strips or shapes, with peel-off backs that expose a precoated adhesive. These are very effective providing the tub is absolutely clean when they are applied. You also can buy rubber mats with suction cups to prevent slips.

But even with all that, every tub should be provided with at least one grab-bar. One can be adequate if it is installed at such an angle that it can be grabbed at different heights. If installed horizontally, there should be two bars — one for anyone using the shower, and one for children. An upper grab-bar, or the upper end of an angled grab-bar, should be about 48" above the bottom of the tub. It should be mounted into the wall studs with 2½" screws. At a lower level, there are soap dishes that build into

Most modern tubs have slip-resistant floors, such as this by American Standard. But for older tubs, use stick-on decals or non-slip rubber mats.

the wall with a built-in grab-bar big enough for a hand, a worthwhile extra precaution.

Be extremely careful of radios and television sets in the bathroom. It's alright to have them there, but never in a position where the controls can be reached by someone in the tub. Any appliances in the bathroom must be properly grounded. A portable electric heater in the bathroom is an invitation to disaster.

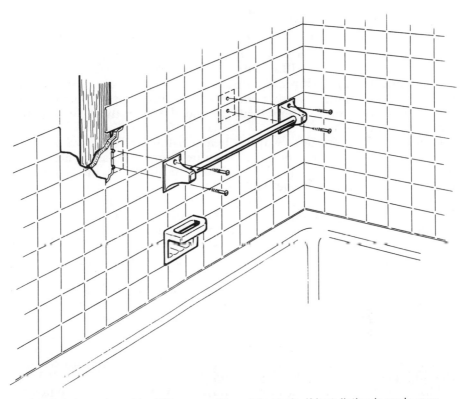

Grab-bar is anchored by 2½" screws driven into studs. If installation is made over ceramic tile, hole should be started with electric drill.

Conserving Energy

There are three ways to save energy in the bathroom. One is the use of fluorescent lights rather than incandescent. Another is a separate heating arrangement. The third is in judicious use of hot water, because your water heater is one of the biggest energy users in the home.

LIGHT AND HEAT. As noted in Chapter 12, you get a lot more light per watt from a fluorescent tube than from an incandescent bulb.

Also as noted in Chapter 12, an infra-red lamp used for heat provides heat for the person in the bathroom without warming the room, and this can represent a considerable saving. A separate heating unit in the bathroom can provide the intermittent heat you need rather than heating the bathroom all the time.

One of the most wasteful ways to heat a bathroom is to turn on a hot shower habitually just for the heat, as is often done in apartments where bathroom heat is not provided. It would be far better to buy your own heat lamp and hang it on the wall.

WATER. The average family of four flushes the toilet 20 times a day, accounting for 40% of all water used in the home. Purchase of a new toilet, such as a Kohler Water-Guard, would save that family 14,600 gallons of water in a year. The other manufacturers of plumbingware have similar water-savers.

That also means 14,600 fewer gallons of sewage, and as many consumers are aware, more and more communities are passing on sewer costs to residents. In some areas sewage rates have risen as much as 170% since 1970.

The technique of putting bricks or bottles into the toilet tank often doesn't work. The toilet is designed for the amount of water it uses, and the gimmicks often result only in extra flushes.

More and more manufacturers are now offering restrictor-type faucets and showerheads. They generally cut the water flow by about 50% or more. Moen, as one example, now is making its "Flow-Rator" standard on all showerheads and faucets. It controls flow to 3 gallons per minute or less at 80 lbs. pressure.

With water-saving showerheads an average family of four, each of whom takes one 5-minute shower per day, can save 21,900 gallons of water per year. This is water that already has burned fuel in the water heater and that contributes to the sewage flow.

Here's how much water it takes:

For a 5-minute shower—30 gallons
For a tub bath—30 gallons
To fill the lav—1-2 gallons
One toilet flush—5-6 gallons

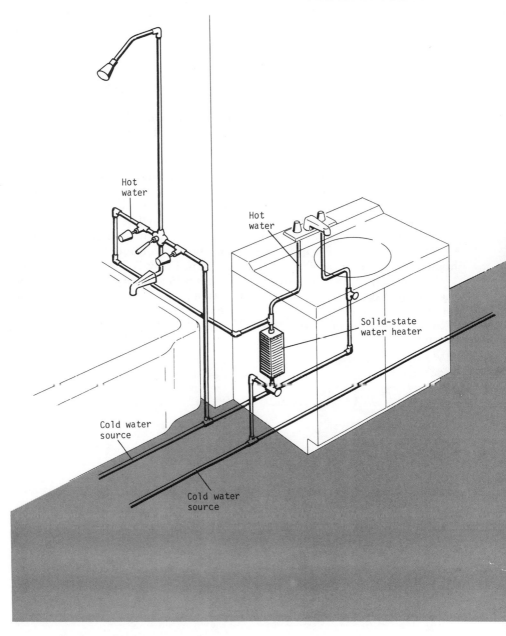

Hot
water

Hot
water

Solid-state
water heater

Cold water
source

Cold water
source

Chronomite's Instant-Flow eliminates the hot water storage tank and its waste,
heats water as it passes through.

Now consider leaks. The Indianapolis Water Co. calculated that a tiny 1/32" stream of water leaking from a faucet will waste 6,550 gallons per month. A 1/4" stream would waste 12,300 gallons per day, or 375,150 gallons per month.

Obviously, it would be prudent to take showers and baths as cool as is comfortable. A cool shower with a restricted flow faucet would save in three ways (including reduced sewage). Another device you may want to consider is the "Instant-Flow" by Chronomite Labs. It applies the principle of the instant-hot-water kitchen dispensers to your hot water needs in the bathroom.

In other words, instead of heating a tankful of water and storing it for your needs, as your water heater does, this device is installed in your cold water line near the point of use, and heats only the water that goes through it. There is no loss of heat from the storage tank or the hot water lines; no wasted energy to keep the tank of water hot.

According to Chronomite, conventional gas water heaters waste 60% to 70% of the energy applied to them, and conventional electric water heaters waste 50% to 60%, whereas Instant-Flow is 98% efficient.

One such Instant-Flow could be installed in a vanity cabinet to serve the lavatory and a nearby tub/shower. (In a kitchen, you would need one for the sink and one for the dishwasher.)

So there are lots of ways to save. The prudent thing is not to ignore any of them.

Nova showerhead by Con-Serv is one of many that save water by cutting flow 50% or more.

HUD Minimum Property Standards

In new home construction or remodeling, builders and contractors are guided by the Minimum Property Standards of the U.S. Department of Housing and Urban Development. This means that even if you do all of the work yourself, you cannot get government-secured loans (FHA, VA, etc.) unless your project is in compliance.

Here are the standard that pertain to the bathroom, with their HUD paragraph numbers.

401-4.2 Baths

a. Each dwelling unit shall have one bathroom containing a lavatory, water closet, and bathtub. In other bathrooms showers may be substituted for bathtubs. Bathrooms shall provide for comfortable access to, and use of, each fixture. Bathrooms shall be convenient to the bedrooms.

b. A seasonal home shall contain at least one lavatory, water closet, and bathtub or shower. The accessories listed in 401-4.2c are not required.

c. Bathrooms shall be provided with the following accessories:
   (1) Grab-bar and soap dish at tub or shower
   (2) Shower curtain rod or enclosure at shower
   (3) Soap dish at lavatory (soap dishs may be integral with the fixture)
   (4) Toilet paper holder at water closet
   (5) Mirror and medicine cabinet or equivalent enclosed storage
   (6) Two towel bars

d. Each half-bath shall be provided with items 3, 4, 5 and 6 in 401-4.2c

e. Stall showers shall have a minimum area of 1024 sq. in. and at least a dimension of 30"

f. Water-impervious wainscot shall be provided at walls around showers or tub-showers to a height of 6' from the bottom of the shower or tub

g. Additional requirements for housing for the elderly
   (1) Bathtubs shall be at least 5' long and shall be provided with at least two grab-bars
   (2) A stall shower with a seat and grab-bars may be provided in lieu of bathtub
   (3) Tub or shower bottom surfaces shall be slip resistant

(4) Grab-bars, towel bars, shower curtain rods and similar bathroom accessories shall be installed to sustain a dead weight of 250 lbs. for five minutes at any point

401-4.3 Laundries
a. In each dwelling unit provide a laundry tray or water and waste piping and space for a clothes washing machine
b. When space for a dryer is provided, it shall be equipped with power supply and vent to the outside
c. For seasonal homes, laundries are not required

401-5.4 Linen storage shall be provided as follows:
a. Minimum shelf area: 10 sq. ft. for two bedrooms, 15 sq. ft. for three or more bedrooms

402-3.2 Minimum doorway widths shall be:
Bathroom, toilet, 2′. (2′8″ for elderly)

402-3.3 A door is required at each entrance to a bedroom, bathroom, and toilet

402-3.4 Locking devices at doors and windows shall be as follows:
d. Bathroom, toilet room, and primary bedroom doors shall be equipped with a privacy lock which can be opened from the outside in an emergency

402-5.1 Each bedroom shall have access to a bathroom without an intervening bedroom, kitchen, or principal living or dining area. Bedrooms shall not afford the only access to a required bathroom. Neither a bedroom nor bathroom shall afford the only access to a habitable room.

402-5.2 For seasonal homes the following shall apply in lieu of the preceding:
a. The only access from a habitable room to another habitable room shall not be through a bedroom or a bathroom
b. The only access from a bedroom to a bathroom shall not be through another bedroom

403-3 Ventilation
Bathroom ventilation shall be the equivalent of 5% of the floor area, or mechanical ventilation shall provide eight air changes per hour

Note: These Minimum Property Standards became effective in 1973. If your house was built before that, your present facilities may not comply and are not affected by the standards. But any new project should comply.

Manufacturers and Associations

Allibert
Raritan Center 423
Edison, NJ 08817

Alsons Corp.
Box 311
Covina, CA 91723

American Home Lighting Institute
230 N. Michigan Ave.
Chicago, IL 60601

American Olean Tile Co.
Lansdale, PA 19446

American Standard Inc.
Box 2003
New Brunswick, NJ 08903

Armstrong Cork Co.
Box 3001
Lancaster, PA 17604

Boise Cascade Corp.
Box 514
Berryville, VA 22611

Broan Mfg. Co.
926 W. State St.
Hartford, WI 53027

Chemcraft Inc.
Box 1086
Elkhart, IN 46514

Chronomite Labs
21011 Figueroa St.
Carson, CA 90745

Con-Serv Inc.
7745 Reinhold Dr.
Cincinnati, OH 45237

Corian Building Products Division
DuPont & Co. Inc.
Wilmington, DE 19898

Duro-Lite Lamps Inc.
17-10 Willow St.
Fair Lawn, NJ 07410

Edgemate Products (Fresh-Face)
Westvaco Corp.
Williamsburg, PA 16693

Eljer Plumbingware Division
Wallace-Murray Corp.
3 Gateway Center
Pittsburgh, PA 15222

Elko Building Supply
Box 2224
Evansville, IN 47711

Formco Inc.
7745 School Rd.
Cincinnati, OH 45242

Formica Corp.
Berdan Ave.
Wayne, NJ 07470

Franciscan Tile
2901 Los Feliz Blvd.
Los Angeles, CA 90039

General Electric Co.
Appliance Park
Louisville, KY 40225

Genova Inc.
7034 E. Court St.
Davison, MI 48423

H&R Johnson
Box 23
Keyport, NJ 07736

Haas Cabinet Co.
625 W. Utica St.
Sellersburg, IN 47172

Hafa
Box 135
301 03 Halmstad
Sweden

Hastings Tile
404 Northern Blvd.
Great Neck, NY 11021

Home Ventilating Institute
4300-L Lincoln Ave.
Rolling Meadows, IL 60008

Intertherm, Inc.
Hot Water Electric Heaters
3800 Park Ave.
St. Louis, MO 63110

IXL Furniture Co.
Route 1
Elizabeth City, NC 27909

Jaclo Inc.
162 Carlton Ave.
Brooklyn, NY 11205

Jacuzzi Whirlpool Bath Inc.
Drawer J
Walnut Creek, CA 94596

J. Josephson Inc.
20 Horizon Blvd.
Hackensack, NJ 07606

Kohler Co.
Kohler, WI 53044

Marlite Division
Masonite Corp.
Dover, OH 44622

Masonite Corp.
29 N. Wacker Dr.
Chicago, IL 60606

Mirrorlite Products
Kamar Corp.
Irvington-on-Hudson, NY 10533

Modern Kitchens of Syracuse
5801 Court Street Rd.
Syracuse, NY 13221

Moen Faucet Division
Stanadyne, Inc.
377 Woodland Ave.
Elyria, OH 44035

Molded Marble Products
Box 219
Menomonee Falls, WI 53051

Nutone Division
Scovill Mfg. Co.
Madison & Red Bank Rds.
Cincinnati, OH 45227

Poggenpohl USA Corp.
222 Cedar Lane
Teaneck, NJ 07666

Quaker Maid Kitchens Division
Tappan Corp.
Route 61
Leesport, PA 19533

Rutt Custom Cabinets Division
Leigh Products, Inc.
Route 23
Goodville, PA 17528

Sherle Wagner Int.
60 E. 57th St.
New York, NY 10022

Steamist Co.
101 Park Ave.
New York, NY 10017

ThermaSol Ltd.
ThermaSol Plaza
Leonia, NJ 07605

Tivoli Industries
1513 E. St. Gertrude Pl.
Santa Ana, CA 92705

Tub-Master Corp.
413 Virginia Dr.
Orlando, FL 32803

Universal-Rundle Corp.
Box 960
New Castle, PA 16103

University of Illinois Small Homes Council
Urbana, IL 61801

Viking Sauna Co.
Box 6298
San Jose, CA 95150

Villeroy & Boch U.S.A., Inc.
Interstate 80 at New Maple Ave.
Pine Brook, NJ 07058

Westinghouse Electric Corp.
Lamps Division
1 Westinghouse Plaza
Bloomfield, NJ 07003

Williams Vanity Division
Leigh Products Inc.
1536 Grant St.
Elkhart, IN 46514

Index